The Passion-Driven Youth Choir

A Guide for Directors of Youth Choirs with 10 to 100 Members

Mark Acker

Abingdon Press

Nashville

THE PASSION-DRIVEN YOUTH CHOIR

Copyright © 2007 by Abingdon Press

This book is printed on acid-free, recycled paper.

ISBN 978-0-687-49224-4

07 08 09 10 11 12 13 14 15 16—10 9 8 7 6 5 4 3 2 1

MANUFACTURED IN THE UNITED STATES OF AMERICA

To the youth
of
Brentwood United Methodist Church
with
love and appreciation

May the God who gives endurance and encouragement give you a spirit of unity as you follow Christ Jesus, so that with one heart and voice *you may glorify the* God and Father of our Lord Jesus Christ. (Romans 15:5 NIV)

CONTENTS

BUILDING A PASSION-DRIVEN CHOIR

CHAPTER ONE

PASSION

Passion is the fire, the desire, the strength of conviction and the drive that sustains the discipline to achieve the vision.[1]
—Stephen Covey

Passion is the lubricant of success.[2]
—Coach Brian Billick

Michael walked into my office one August afternoon, introduced himself, and said "I was wondering if I could go on the retreat this weekend. I might want to join the choir." Michael was about to begin his senior year in high school and was friends with a number of youth in the choir; he had grown up in our church, but had never become involved in the choirs or youth group. The fall back-to-school choir retreat that we were about to begin was held each year at a beautiful camp with ski boats, horses, and other outdoor activities. Our retreat would include lots of rehearsal, small group and worship time, as well as significant time for recreation. It was designed to attract potential new choir members as well as to help jump-start our year. Michael attended the retreat, participated fully, and by the end was hooked on being a part of the choir. Michael was faithful to rehearsals and to being a part of the choir each Sunday morning over the next ten months. He was also a part of the choir tour in July, in which we sang at a homeless shelter, two schools for special needs children, an inner-city child-care facility, two retirement homes, an inner-city church, and a suburban church. In addition to these concerts, the choir worshiped together each day, the seniors were honored at Senior Night, and we stayed overnight at a monastery, where we attended worship and talked with the monks.

Three years later, Michael's mother, who had battled cancer for many years, was close to dying. On the night before her death, Michael and several young people from the choir joined hands around the bed of his mother, and sang Douglas Wagner's "May the Peace of the Lord," the benediction that the choir sings at the end of each Sunday's worship service:

> May the peace of the Lord go always with you.
> May the light of His love shine bright.
> May the peace of the Lord glow warm within you,
> and go with you from this place.[3]

On the day before the funeral, many people gathered at the funeral home to greet the family and to pay their respects to Michael's mother. The casket had been purchased by Michael and his family from the monastery that we had visited on choir tour; because of the spirituality that Michael had experienced at the monastery during our overnight visit on tour, Michael wanted his mother to be buried in one of the simple but beautiful caskets that are made by the monks at the monastery.

Michael spoke at the funeral, gave a loving tribute to his mother, and told how much it had meant to her that he was a part of the choir his senior year. Then Michael walked over to the choir loft and joined many of his friends, as well as current members of the choir, as they sang Linda Spencer's "Wings of the Dawn."

I am in awe of the ways in which God used the experiences of one year in the choir to influence Michael's life in very dramatic ways, and for the ways in which the events surrounding the death of his mother were a witness to the passionate power of Michael's experiences in the choir.

The story is not always this wonderful, of course, for there are often many challenges in youth choirs that can sometimes result in youth falling through the cracks or not having a positive experience. But in a great youth choir, many youth, like Michael, experience something they cannot get anywhere else, and they are never the same again. And it is because of Michael, and all the teenagers who have been, and will be, a part of our choirs, that we do this thing called "leading a youth choir."

My Story

For over nineteen years (1984–2004) I served as director of music, worship, and the arts at Brentwood United Methodist Church in Brentwood, Tennessee, a suburb of Nashville. During this time, the church grew from 2,000 members to over 5,000 members. The youth choir ministry, which had a strong tradition prior to my arrival, also grew to include approximately 175 to 200 youth in grades 7 through 12 who were active in choir each year. Our division was originally a choir for seventh and eighth graders, and a choir for ninth through twelfth graders (this is the way in which the schools were divided). After a few years of growth, it became clear that in spite of the school division, we needed to change the way in which the choirs were grouped. After meeting with both youth and parent leaders and youth ministry staff, the decision was made to create a choir for seventh through ninth grade, and a choir for tenth through twelfth grade. After some initial "shock," this system began to work well; it created a "junior high choir" with ninth-grade leaders, and boys who could sing bass, and it created a "senior high choir" that was more manageable in size. Generally, the older choir sang at least three Sundays each month as worship leaders in the 8:30 A.M. worship service, and the younger choir sang one Sunday each month as the worship choir for the 8:30 A.M. worship service. After a few years, Beth Teegarden, associate director of music, became director of the younger group, and I remained as director of the older group.

This book has been in process for many years. Most of the core material was written while I was still serving at Brentwood, so most of the suggestions presented in this book are based on the youth choir ministry there. Although the choirs at Brentwood were large, almost everything in this book is usable or adaptable for choirs of seven or twenty or whatever small or large number of members your choir may include.

Some material in this book is written from the vantage point of hindsight and of my experiences in churches since leaving Brentwood. Both from my personal experiences, and from the stories that directors have shared with me over the years, I know that it can be challenging to begin a youth choir in a place where there is no youth choir tradition, where the youth choir tradition is negative, where various situations in the past or present affect the beginning of a new director's ministry, or where youth or adult leaders are less than totally supportive. The director's age can also affect the nuances of the way in which a youth choir ministry is led. Time is a great healer, however, and new directors and churches must sometimes be patient as seeds are planted and given a chance to grow.

The arrival of a new director is an opportunity for a church and for youth ministry leaders to be the church; that is, it is a time in which a decision can be made to welcome and support this new person, because that's what we do in the church. And, of course, youth choir directors who have served in the same church for a number of years must also model and encourage acceptance and support of new youth ministry staff.

"Successful" youth choirs happen because of many things, including traditions, church health, youth ministry, the community in which the church sits, the support of youth and adult leaders, and other factors unique to each situation. But, in the end, in spite of any external influences, a successful youth choir will rely heavily on the work and dedication of a capable and passionate director.

The choirs at Brentwood did not grow because I am "cool." I am, in most ways, the opposite of what most would view as cool.

But as the director of the youth choir, I was passionate about building a youth choir ministry that was strong both musically and spiritually, I cared about the youth as individuals, and I worked hard. The choir also grew because some adult persons with influence and teenagers with influence made the decision to support the youth choir, and they grew because of supportive youth ministers, great accompanists, and encouraging pastors. And we were lucky. Truthfully, in the end, it was a God-thing all the way; there were too many "breaks," too many things that worked out, and too many mistakes on my part for it to have not been a God-thing.

So this book is simply a sharing of things that I think are important, things that I found helpful, and things that I wish I had known earlier in my ministry. It has been written because I believe that what you and I do as directors of youth choirs is a great gift and a great responsibility, and because I believe in the power and importance of young people singing their faith.

Caring About the Needs of Teenagers

Recognizing and responding to the needs of young people is the first step in building a youth choir that is a *ministry*. This is what I have come to believe:

- Every person longs to be known and to be accepted in a group.
- Every person will be enriched when they connect with God.
- Every person will experience joy when they make a difference in the lives of others.
- Most every youth will find a connection when they "find their voice," and experience the power of choral singing and using their God-given instrument.
- Every person grows through commitment to something "bigger than ourselves."
- Young people need adults, in addition to parents, who love and support them.

The Purpose of a Youth Choir

Every director must answer the question "What is the purpose of this choir?" For some, it is music education, for some it is to help young people learn to love the "classics" of choral literature, for some it is all about spiritual formation, and for some, it is to provide a fun environment for teenagers.

The power of the church youth choir lies in the reality that through it we can offer a truly holistic experience for teenagers. In fact, we can offer an experience that they *cannot get anywhere else*[4] —a musical, social, and spiritual experience that can impact their lives forever.

The church youth choir director must offer music education, vocal and choral training, spiritual formation, and an accepting and joyful environment for teenagers. We also must be aware of the theology that we are teaching through the texts that the choir sings. We need to consider how the choir can expand the worldview of the young people in the group through the kinds of places that we might go to sing, such as a prison, a homeless mission, a community AIDS awareness event, or a school for special needs persons. And we need to remember that being a part of a group can help us learn how to live in community—how to love and accept one another, how to care for those with emotional or physical challenges, and how to take seriously the challenge to be the hands and voice of Christ in the world.

I believe that we as directors are called to *excellence* in music— not sloppy, or "good enough" because it is church or because this is a youth choir, or because it's more important for the choir to be doing things other than rehearsing. But I also believe that the purpose of the church youth choir is ultimately deeper than the music, and that through a holistic youth choir experience, young people can connect with God and with one another. They can know what it means to connect with the people of this world who are "different" from those in the bubble in which most of us live and can grow to have a lifelong connection with the power of worship and prayer in their lives.

Passionate Singing

As directors, we must believe in and constantly work at offering choral experiences that connect youth with passionate music making. A number of years ago, Donald Neuen, the great American conductor, began a rehearsal with our youth choir with this dialogue:

"Who made his piano?" (People in a factory)

"How much is it worth?" ($10,000 or more)

"How would you feel if I jumped up and down on it?" (That would be bad.)

"Who made some of the best violins that some members of the symphony play?" (Some are handmade by craftsmen.)

"How much is it worth?" (Some might be worth $50,000 or more.)

"How would you feel if I slammed it down on the floor?" (Mad)

"Who made your voice?" (God)

"How much is it worth?" (Priceless)

"How do you think God feels when we treat our voices badly?" (Not good)

Then Don Neuen said: "Our voice is the only instrument that God made. That is why I believe that choral singing is God's favorite music. What a privilege, honor, and responsibility it is for each of us to sing together in this choir."

The room was filled with the silence of a wonderful aha! moment. And beautiful, spirit-filled music was created in the moments that followed.

A Passionate Director

A great youth choir ministry—one that speaks to needs of the whole person—needs a director who is:
- **Passionate.** It takes a director who is passionate about the *power* of faith, the church, and music.

- **Energetic.** It takes a director who is willing to invest time writing notes to youth, in planning all aspects of the choir ministry, and in supporting youth outside of choir rehearsal.
- **Visionary.** It takes a director who can look beyond today and dream the kind of youth choir ministry that "fits" this church, and the kind of music ministry that will be a powerful force in that church, community, and indeed in the world.
- **Skilled.** It takes a director who knows how to teach youth to sing, and who is skilled at helping the group to be an excellent choir.
- **Committed.** It takes a director who is committed to helping build a choir that is uniquely a church choir, and to building a choir that makes a difference musically, spiritually, and socially in the lives of those who participate.

A Passionate Church Community

Great youth choirs are formed by supportive and passionate churches that understand the need to connect young people with the power of all kinds of music. Erwin McManus says: "Somewhere on the road, we seem to have lost our love of beauty for beauty's sake, as if somehow God did not indulge in this kind of triviality. Those who worship the God of creation must never forget how beauty reflects both God and His values. The church's birthright is to be the fountainhead of creativity and human potential." McManus adds:

> The church can become the place where the great artists of our time paint their first strokes and the great musicians sing their first notes. The church can become the place where the great thinkers and the great scholars and the great writers emerge.
> The church can become the environment in which the future's poets and film directors, dancers, and doctors grow up in community and learn that their talents are gifts from God.

The future leaders will come from somewhere. Shouldn't it be from the church?[5]

Ultimately, when passion-filled teenagers connect with a passionate director, passionate singing, and a passionate faith community, they will experience *something they cannot get anywhere else*—a musical, social, and spiritual experience that connects youth to a purpose greater than themselves. When this happens, a passion-driven youth choir has been set in motion, and the lives of all who are touched by this ministry will never be the same.

Notes

1. Stephen Covey, *The 8th Habit: From Effectiveness to Greatness* (New York: Free Press, 2004), p. 66.
2. Brian Billick, *Competitive Leadership* (Chicago: Triumph Books, 2001), p. 6.
3. Douglas Wagner, "May the Peace of the Lord," Hope Publishing Company, catalogue no. A-606.
4. A concept that I first learned from Bishop Joe E. Pennel, Jr.
5. Erwin McManus, *An Unstoppable Force: Daring to Become the Church God Had in Mind* (Loveland, CO: Group Publishing, 2001), p. 183.

STAGES

The greatest good we can do for others is not to share our riches with them but to reveal theirs to them.

—Anonymous

"I didn't want to go to choir in the beginning. But when you sent me a note saying you wanted me to join, you changed my life."
—Letter from a former youth choir member

Consider the following four typical youth choir members: **Brett** is a ninth grader in the senior high choir. This is his first year in choir and he attends mainly because his best friend invited him. Although Brett participates, he does so with a less-than-eager attitude, and he frequently talks with those sitting around him.

Cathy joined the choir six months ago. At first she came because her parents encouraged her. Now, however, Cathy looks forward to each week's rehearsal and finds that she really enjoys singing in the choir. She has even mentioned to her mother that she would like to take a few voice lessons.

Paul is a mature high school junior who participates in numerous school and church activities. Paul is serious about his faith and often has a devotion and prayer time. Paul has been on choir tour twice and knows the choir can have a positive influence on persons who hear it sing. Paul reaches out to others in the choir and encourages them to give their best effort each week in rehearsal.

Amy is a quiet leader. Her peers respect her. Her relationship with God is very important. Amy wants the choir to be a great musical and spiritual experience for all of the members of the group. She reaches out to others and faithfully prays for both youth and adult leaders. She also is an excellent singer and a leader in the alto section.

Brett, Cathy, Paul, and Amy are examples of the variety of youth found in most church youth choirs. Each young person comes to the choir experience from a very different place musically, spiritually, and emotionally. Recognizing where each youth is in his or her musical, emotional, and spiritual journey is important and helpful for adult leaders. By understanding these stages of growth in young people, leaders are better able to minister to individuals, and are able to know what needs to be done to move each person, and the group, to the next level of musical and spiritual growth.

The Four Stages

1. ATTENDING

The youth in this group participate either because of friends, parental pressure, or the payoff (like a trip). The faith and choral experience basically eludes them. Work to connect these youth through personal contact by adult and youth leaders.

2. INVOLVED

For members of this group, the faith and choral experience begins to have an impact. Youth begin to see the value of the faith message and choral experience. Respond to these youth by affirming their participation and by affirming their questions and interest.

3. COMMITTED

These youth have made a faith commitment and want their lives to reflect their faith. They understand the importance of discipline in the choral experience and see that the experience of singing has an impact on singers and listeners. Involve these youth in leadership, covenant groups, and hold them accountable for leadership in the choir and in spiritual disciplines.

4. LEADER

Leaders are the peer-mentors of the youth group and choir. These youth know and are able to live out the essence of the Christian message. Adult leaders need to personally mentor these youth, hold them accountable to the groups' vision of ministry, and give them opportunities to share their developed gifts in specific ways.

Understanding the Stages

Understanding the stages leads to balance in ministry. Through all that happens in both youth groups and in choirs, we must be sensitive to the youth who are in each of these stages. It is important to help each youth to grow and to move, if possible, to the next level of development.

Movement in the Stages

Age and grade in school have little specific relevance to the stage that a young person is in, and teenagers will move from stage to stage ("forward" and "backward") during their time in the youth group and choir. For example, almost everyone in the group will move to deeper levels of commitment and skill during times such as choir tours and retreats. Be ready to respond and to help young people during these special times.

Pictures of the Group

For many choirs, the beginning of a new year may look like this:

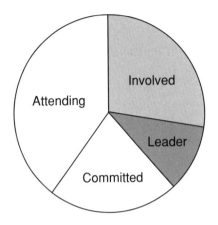

Because the majority of the choir is in the attending and involved stages, the beginning of the year may need to focus on extra rehearsals, a retreat, and with the director meeting one-on-one with each member of the choir. Those in the *committed* group can be mentored and can become choir leaders.

As the year progresses, some of the *attending* members will drop away, some will move into the *involved* group, and, of course, some will stay in the *attending* group. Mid-year, the group picture might look like this:

Mid-year emphasis may need to be focused on the *involved* and *committed* groups. A class in vocal development, music reading, or a leadership prayer group all may be important programs to offer at this time in the year.

As the choir year concludes, and particularly after peak experiences such as a tour, the picture of the group

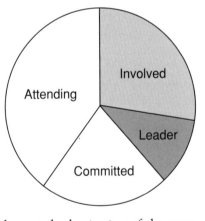

likely will be totally different than at the beginning of the year. The musical and spiritual achievements of the choir have influenced the young people in the choir, and have helped move the majority of the choir members into the *committed* and *leader* groups. The musical, spiritual, and emotional journey of the choir year can have a powerful influence on the lives of teenagers with whom we work.

Stages of Teenage Growth

For the choir experience to be all that it can be, and for our ministry with youth to be at its best, we must be constantly aware of each youth as a total person. Changes and struggles that are a normal part of a teenager's life will also affect the choir experience and the choir ministry.

CHARACTERISTICS OF JUNIOR HIGH YOUTH
Ages 11-15/Grades 7-8
- Are intellectually concrete, limited to experience
- Are very emotional, erratic
- Have a short attention span, activity-oriented
- Are self-oriented—key question: "Do you like me?"
- Have a preoccupation with physical body
- Have love/hate relationships
- Understand value judgments in black or white
- Display rebellion in brief, sharp pulses
- Are more dependent
- Run in packs
- Have short-term relationships
- Understand God as church or group
- Understand church as a lot of people who do certain things

GENERAL CHARACTERISTICS OF SENIOR HIGH YOUTH
Ages 15-18/Grades 9-12
- Are developing intellectual curiosity, find pleasure in dealing with ideas; are able to think abstractly and generalize principles
- Are more stable, more in control of emotions
- Have a longer attention span; love to discuss ideas
- Are more oriented to the larger world
- Are developing an understanding of sexual self in interpersonal relationships
- May have periods of disagreement with parents over car, dating, and job
- Can see shades of gray

- May begin sexual experimentation and sexual relationships
- Display less intense but more sustained rebellion
- Are more independent
- Seek out individuals through dating and special friends
- See God as individual and personal
- See church as community, a group, and the body of Christ

Ten Suggestions for Relating to Youth

1. Be yourself! Better to be an "honest geek" than to be a "cool fake."
2. Be professional. Be the adult.
3. Be understanding. Youth have many demands on their time. Roll with their schedule when necessary.
4. Be vulnerable. Share a little of yourself. Admit your mistakes. Be real.
5. Be available. Be in your office before and after rehearsals and at other times.
6. Challenge them. Demand the best.
7. Laugh. Let youth know that you enjoy being with them.
8. Work closely with youth and adult leaders. Build a core group that helps you lead.
9. Let your faith shine through what you say and do. Youth are hungry for a consistent faith role model.
10. Care about the youth as individuals and find ways to connect with each person.

CHAPTER THREE

BUILDING

*The most important way to forge a winning team is to call on
the players' need to connect with something larger than themselves.*[1]
—Phil Jackson in *Sacred Hoops*

*"I still can't believe that John and several of his super-cool, hip,
do-our-thing, sneak smokes and beer, spoiled-by-too-much-money
friends somehow found themselves at church every Sunday morning at
8:00 to sing in choir. And tears come easily because I know that many
of the young people in the choir loft now will be touched
forever by this experience—and they don't even know it yet."*
—Letter from the father of a former choir member

The nonmusical factors that most influence youth choirs
today are in reality the same factors that influence adults.
These factors are often the enemy of church youth choirs
and, ultimately, of young people themselves:

1. The "traditional" family is no longer the "normal" family unit. Typical examples include both parents working, single-parent homes, and blended families.

2. Society promotes an attitude of individualism. Youth and their parents are often more concerned with meeting personal wants rather than with making long-term commitments to serving others.

3. Sunday is no longer church day. School and community groups now regularly schedule activities on Sunday.

4. Leisure and sports are a priority. From elementary age children's teams to professional leagues, sports teams are the royalty of our time, and athletes are today's most honored and rewarded persons. High school athletics demand tremendous time commitments. Churches in cities with pro football teams are affected by Sunday games.

5. Money and winning are primary. Young people often equate happiness with acquiring things and with winning, not with serving others.

6. People are searching for meaning in the wrong places. Youth and their parents frequently search for meaning or mask their emotional pain through acquiring things (like clothes and cars), substance abuse (alcohol, drugs, and tobacco), inappropriate sexual activity, and job and achievement addiction.

Building Blocks

Building blocks to a great youth choir ministry include:

1. Have high expectations. Set a vision for musical quality, commitment of the youth to rehearsals and performances, outstanding appearance, and positive behavior. Regular participation in worship leadership—every week or twice monthly—is a high expectation to which youth will respond.

2. Strive for a high quality "product." The choir must sound good when it performs. Choose music that is appropriate musically and textually, work hard in rehearsals, and sound great in performance.

3. Be an active recruiter. Recruiting is a never-ending part of a director's work. Involve youth leaders in the recruitment process.

4. Offer awesome retreats and tours. Provide opportunities for incredible musical, spiritual, and social experiences on retreats and tours. Invest whatever it takes to make retreats and tours great. Being great has less to do with where you go, but rather with the musical, social, and spiritual experiences of the events. It also has to do with connecting young people with the hurting, poor, or forgotten people of our world, because teenagers are often passionate about making a difference in the lives of others.

5. **Develop meaningful rituals and traditions.** Young people love and value rituals and traditions. Develop worship and group-building traditions that are unique and meaningful to your group.

6. **Intentionally connect the youth minister and the senior pastor to the youth choir.** Henri Nouwen, in his book *In the Name of Jesus*, reminds us that Jesus sent his disciples out in pairs. Nouwen says: "Whenever we minister together, it is easier for people to recognize that we do not come in our own name, but in the name of the Lord Jesus who sends us."[2] The same partnership can be true for youth choir directors and youth ministers and senior pastors. Modeling love, respect, and support among the youth choir director and the youth minister and the senior pastor is a win-win for everyone.

7. **Value the time and commitment youth give to the choir.** Respect the time that youth give to the choir, and be sensitive to the many other commitments that are a part of every teenager's life.

8. **Build a "happy" atmosphere in the music area and create an atmosphere that encourages all youth to feel welcome in choir.** Food is always a great way to welcome people—cookies as they arrive for rehearsals, doughnuts when they sing for early Sunday services. Pictures of the youth choir "in action," and a room organized and ready for rehearsal or warm-up are other ways of saying "this is important—I'm glad that you are here."

9. **Be a caring director.** Find ways of showing care to individuals, such as attending school plays, concerts, and athletic events. Send cards or call on birthdays. Write notes on mailings.

10. **Make church choir an experience that is unique to the church.** In the church youth choir, achieving a great choral sound joins hands with using music and the choir experience as

a means of worship and faith development. A spiritual emphasis is never an excuse, however, for poor musicianship. Make the most of the opportunity in church choir to discuss the meaning of texts, and to form a "faith family" as well as a "choral family."

Beginnings

Every situation is unique, but consider the following suggestions as you begin to form a new youth choir:

1. Meet with the senior pastor and your supervisor to determine their expectations for the youth choir. In addition to listening to their thoughts, share your own vision for the youth choir ministry.

2. Meet with the youth minister or adults who are responsible for the youth program. Ask for their suggestions and help. Discuss your plans so that the music and youth departments are "on the same page."

3. Meet with a small group of youth who are leaders. Share your initial plans and your passions with them. Ask for their input and their leadership in beginning the youth choir.

4. Recruit youth for an overnight retreat. On the retreat, get to know the youth, sing great music, have fun, and offer meaningful worship.

Recruiting

Here are ten practical suggestions for recruiting youth for the choir:

1. Young people are their own best advertisement. Encourage them to bring their friends to be a part of the choir. Organize a group of youth leaders to call every youth who is on the church rolls; a "party" using numerous phones at the church, followed by a dinner is a great way to involve youth in recruiting.

2. Personal contact by the director is critical. Make phone calls, write personal notes, and meet youth at church and school events.

3. Plan a fall kick-off retreat at a great camp. Recruit as many youth as possible to attend. They may agree to go because of the fun activities provided at the camp, but they will come back home having experienced the power of music, worship, and relationships, and will now be hooked on the choir experience.

4. Keep the church aware of the choir ministry through newsletters, posters, bulletins, and so on. Schedule the choir to sing at as many events as possible.

5. Work to make the choir "new member friendly." Assign officers to greet and sit with new members, and consider having a big brother/little sister program in the choir.

6. While on choir tour, send handwritten postcards to prospects and to youth who will be moving up to the grade eligible for youth choir.

7. Design creative mail-outs for recruitment.

8. Have respected youth speak in worship and to the youth group about the youth choir.

9. Never give up on a youth. Without nagging, continue to let a youth know that he or she is wanted in the choir.

10. Connect with choral and band teachers at local high schools. Attend concerts by these groups, and enlist these teachers as helpers in recruiting youth for the church choir.

Ideas to Keep Youth Choir Members Coming Back

1. Have a well-planned rehearsal, organized for optimum learning with hard work, a positive attitude, a sense of accomplishment, and a good ending.

2. Choirs need constant goals and a sense of purpose. Regular worship participation is important. Tours are also excellent goals.

3. Send a letter to new choir members letting them know that you are glad that they have joined the choir. In the letter, include

choir plans and goals for the year as well as expectations of members.

4. Have a choir officer call all new choir members. A personal phone call makes the new member feel connected to the group.

5. Be an adult friend. Let youth know that you care about them, not because they are members of the choir but because you really like them.

6. Have a retreat at the beginning of the choir year. Include musical, spiritual, and group-building activities.

7. Contact youth who miss more than two rehearsals in a row.

8. Be aware of choir members who seem to be lonely or discouraged. Let them know that you care.

9. Don't give up on the "problem" youth. The teenagers who make the most noise or hassle you the most may end up being your strongest choir members after they test you. They could need a little extra love and attention.

10. Have a bowling night for seniors and new members of the choir. Assign the seniors to specific new members for the night.

11. In the spring of the year, prepare the choir calendar and gather school schedules for the coming year. During the summer, keep working to add special dates like proms, homecomings, choir and band concerts, trips, and other important dates. Create one master calendar, and try to avoid conflicts with important school dates.

12. Be understanding when there are conflicts that the members of the choir cannot avoid.

13. Avoid extra rehearsals. Make your weekly rehearsal as productive as possible.

14. Be supportive of your young people's involvement in school choir, band, plays, sports, and other activities. Attend the big events presented by these groups. Your support ultimately will help your teenager to be even more supportive of church choir.

15. Invest in seniors. Instill in seniors that this is the year to give back. Even if they are "tired" of choir, this is the year to give the younger members of the group what the seniors of the past gave to them. A strong senior class that is faithful to choir helps

set the standard for everyone in the group. Give seniors up-front leadership roles.

Traditions

Traditions are events that happen repeatedly, and become a part of the ethos of a group. There is great power in *good* traditions. Good traditions are affirming to the entire group and lead to connecting with the purpose of the group. Now, more than ever, groups must be careful that "traditions" are completely appropriate, that they do not make anyone uncomfortable, and that they are not simply one more way of recognizing "popular" youth.

Good traditions for youth choir ministry at Brentwood UMC included:

Trust Walk. At the beginning of the year retreat in August, each new member of the choir was blindfolded, and guided by an older member of the choir. At a camp that we used for many years, the walk took about ten to fifteen minutes, and led to an outdoor worship area. When the blindfolds came off, everyone was looking at fifty or more candles burning, some in the shape of a cross. During our sharing time, older members of the choir told what the choir had meant to them, and we all shared our commitment to be a family in the coming year.

Seniors. We honor seniors in a meaningful way on choir tour, we recognize them at home concert, and we look to them for leadership throughout the year.

Former Members at Home Concert. At the end of home concert, all former members are invited to come forward to join the choir in singing Douglas Wagner's "May the Peace of the Lord."

Christmas Eve 11:00 P.M. Service. This is the service in which college students who are home sing. Some adults and high school youth also sing, but it is primarily former members of the choir who pack the loft for this service.

Communication

Constant communication with youth involved in choir is very important. We must say it, say it again, and say it again! There are three things that we must constantly work at communicating:

1. Letting our singers know what's happening (when and where kind of things);

2. Reminding our singers of why we are doing what we're doing (reminding them of the big picture—the spiritual dimensions);

3. Telling our singers that they are important as persons, not just as members of the choir.

WEEKLY COMMUNICATION

Teenagers appreciate weekly mail—both snail mail and e-mail. These messages focus on letting singers know dates and times of upcoming events, reminding them of the spiritual dimension of our work, and affirming their involvement. We also may use these messages to challenge them. Creative artwork and graphics help make these notes effective. Consider writing a personal note to each youth on mail-outs. Use the church newsletter and youth ministry newsletter to reinforce all information that youth choir members and their parents need to know. Phone trees can also be an effective way of keeping youth and parents informed.

PICTURE WALL

Nothing tells the story better than large pictures of the choir, posted in the hall or in the rehearsal room, or in the youth ministry area. Includes pictures of the group performing, pictures from retreats, recreation, worship, and pictures of small groups of youth in the choir who are enjoying being together.

COMMUNICATING WITH YOUTH INDIVIDUALLY

Here are some suggestions for one-on-one communication opportunities:

1. Call choir members on their birthdays. If you can't do this, send them a card.

2. Attend activities in which your youth are involved, such as ball games, plays, and other events.
3. Host smaller groups, such as seniors or other classes for burgers in your home.
4. Host a Super Bowl party.
5. Be present at youth ministry events simply to "hang out."
6. Be available thirty minutes before and after rehearsals for visiting with youth.
7. Write notes to individuals prior to big events in which they are involved (such as school plays, big games, or concerts).
8. Write short notes on mailings.
9. Write (not type) letters to new members letting them know of your happiness that they have joined the choir.
10. If your youth ministry has a small group ministry, offer to facilitate a group.

Choir Officers

Choir officers are an important part of leadership and communication in youth choirs. There are many models for officers, but I have found it best to have male and female co-presidents elected by the entire choir. These two leaders are supported by a class representative of each grade level in the choir. This group of students become the leadership team for the choir, and help plan events such as retreats and tours, and take the lead in recruiting and integrating new persons into the choir.

Notes

1. Phil Jackson and Hugh Delehanty, *Sacred Hoops: Spiritual Lessons of a Hardwood Warrior* (New York: Hyperion, 1995), p. 123.
2. Henri J. M. Nouwen, *In the Name of Jesus: Reflections on Christian Leadership* (New York: Crossroad, 1989), p. 41.

MAKING THE MOST OF THE REHEARSAL

CHAPTER FOUR

COMMUNITY IN REHEARSALS

*Coming together is a beginning; keeping together is
progress; working together is success.*[1]

—Henry Ford

Deep in their souls, young people are searching. When they consider the decision to join the youth choir, they are hoping to meet three needs in a church choir rehearsal:

- **Community.** The need to connect with others.
- **Wholeness through musical excellence.** The need for moments of transcendence through music. In the minds of the singers, two things must happen: (1) This sounds great. I'm proud to be a part of this choir; and (2) I am emotionally and spiritually moved as I sing in this group.
- **Spirituality.** The need to reconnect with God's Spirit in their lives.

Community Through Sharing Our Story

Weston Noble, the conductor of the Nordic Choir at Luther College for more than fifty years, taught me the importance and power of community. A number of years ago, prior to an amazing concert by the Nordic Choir, the choir sat in our choir room as a member of the choir told his life story—growing up, family, how he came to be a part of the Nordic Choir, his struggles, his hopes, and what he loved about being a part of the choir. I was very surprised at the amount of time this young man took to "tell his story," especially just prior to a concert.

The next morning, Westin Noble told me that storytelling is a tradition of the Nordic Choir. The young people are brutally honest in their sharing with the choir, he told me. And at the conclusion of the story, each member of the choir comes and hugs the person who has spoken. Then he made this amazing statement: "This is why the choir sounds the way that they sound."

We now have a person in the choir share their story during most rehearsals. To make it easier, and to keep a basic time limit, I have a list of questions that I suggest each person talk about. Some are very open and honest when they share, and some are not. But whether or not the person sharing is open, hearing the stories of others is powerful.

Hearing other persons in the choir share about their favorite song, their favorite memory from choir tour, and how choir affects them spiritually is a great way to keep passion for music and for people alive in the choir. After the person has shared, one person comes to the front, places his hand on the person who has shared, and says a prayer on behalf of the entire choir.

Questions for a Brief Life Story in Youth Choir

1. Name, school, grade in school
2. Family—are you close to your family?
3. What activities are important to you? (sports, band, job)
4. What is the most challenging thing about your life, or challenging event in your life; or what has been the most awesome experience of your life?
5. Whom do you admire, and why?
6. When have you felt the closest to God?

7. What is your favorite choir tour memory?
8. What is your favorite choir song, and why?
9. What is your favorite Scripture, and why?

Additional Ways to Build Community

Other ways to build community include:
1. Have a weekly "Who Is This?" contest. Read a series of statements about a member of the choir, and let people guess who it is.
2. Serve food. Consider having a different parent provide cookies each week for rehearsal, or periodically having pizza after rehearsal.
3. Have each class to your home for burgers and games. Invite seniors one month, juniors another month.
4. Give a local concert, and rent a bus to get there. There is something about being on a bus and going somewhere that helps to build community and purpose.

Note

1. Quoted in Brian Billick, *Competitive Leadership*, p. 165.

CHAPTER FIVE

MUSICAL EXCELLENCE IN REHEARSALS

The great leaders are like the best conductors—they reach beyond the notes to reach the magic in the players.[1]

—Blaine Lee

Selection of Music

Careful selection of music for the youth choir is crucial. The texts must be theologically sound and speak to teenagers. The melodies and harmonic parts must be appropriate for the voice of a teenager. Most important, look for music of *all music periods* that is compelling—music that will *engage* young people through a great text, beautiful harmony, or rhythmic vitality.

Score Study

1. Learn everything about the score, including:
   - Tempo
   - Dynamics

- Rhythm
- Articulation
- Phrasing
- Diction
- Melodic and rhythmic themes
- Historical period of the music

2. Develop a system for marking scores, such as a yellow high-light—every instruction given on the score; a blue highlight—words that you expect to work with for proper diction or word stress; a red pencil to mark dynamics; and a black pencil to mark phrases. Simplicity is important.

Interpreting the Text

Consider the following components when preparing each anthem:

1. What does the music say? Consider the musical elements that the composer uses to effectively set the text, such as harmony, repetition, or rhythm.
2. What does the text mean?
3. In what historical context was the text written?
4. What does it say to us today?
5. How does the music support the text?
6. Was this anthem written for a specific occasion or in memory of an important event?
7. Who is the composer? What aspects of his/her life are important to know?

Suggestions for Rehearsals

1. Don Neuen says: Be ready to teach and inspire.[2]
2. Create contrasts in the order of pieces (fast-slow, difficult-easy, and so on).
3. Talk as little as possible; sing as much as possible.
4. Use sectional rehearsals regularly.

5. Be positive and enthusiastic.
6. Print the rehearsal order on a blackboard.
7. In each rehearsal, sing something unaccompanied. Having a repertoire of several *a cappella* anthems is a gift to our singers—they will love these pieces best and will sing them in small groups at unique times!
8. Speak to the singer's imagination and spirit.
9. Rehearse difficult passages without the piano and without the director singing with the choir.
10. Know the two or three most important things that need to be accomplished in a rehearsal, and go for it!
11. Consider using adults in the rehearsal. These adults are not disciplinarians; they are persons who care about the youth, who help with the logistics of the choir, and who sing in rehearsals.
12. Study the music ahead of time. Know how you want a piece of music to sound. Practice conducting difficult passages before rehearsal. Have a teaching plan for each anthem.
13. Use sports analogies or motivation ideas from books by coaches.
14. Try practicing in a circle.
15. Be human—admit your mistakes, laugh.
16. Have a warm-up time and a "cool-down" time. Like exercise, there needs to be a time in rehearsals to get the body and voice ready, then a time of working hard, and then a "cool-down" time.
17. Start and end on time.
18. Have a sign-in sheet or other method of taking attendance that does not take time away from the rehearsal.
19. Have the youth president take part in each rehearsal, such as making the announcements or saying the prayer.
20. Move people or sections to new positions to create variety in the rehearsal and to achieve choral blend.

Voice Checks

Consider meeting individually with each member of the choir. Part of the purpose of this meeting is to do a vocal check; but even more important, this meeting provides an opportunity to get to know each youth and to know of the passions and concerns of his or her life. The Youth Choir Information Form is useful as one meets with each choir member (see page 52). In many churches, it may be helpful to offer private voice lessons or a voice class.

Musical Communication

We sing in worship and in concerts to communicate—to connect with the listener. Don Neuen says that a choral singer must be one-third musician, one-third technician, and one-third dramatic actor. Singers must be extroverts when they sing![3] Great choral sound is achieved through:

1. Good posture. Have singers stretch arms over their heads, then slowly put them down, keeping the same expansion feeling. Heads must be up.

2. Resonance. Singing on a "cold air" breath, allowing for relaxed and open throat, and a relaxed and alert body.

3. Choral Energy. Energy in the sound is achieved through a sense of stretching and pulling the line with energy and good breath support. Energy is achieved only when the whole body is supporting the voice.

4. Diction. Tall vowels, crisp consonants, diphthongs, word stress

5. Articulation. Legato, non-legato

6. Dynamics. Don Neuen says, "Sing the heck out of louds and sing the heck out of softs."[4]

7. Mechanical Accuracy. Know the notes!

8. Blend. The appropriate choral sound from each section combining to form a beautiful whole.

9. Expression. Emotion in the sound is achieved through musical treatment of the text and the music.

10. Intonation. Bull's-eye pitch.

Baggage in Rehearsals

As conductors, we need to be aware of the emotional baggage that we can bring into the rehearsal room, as well as being sensitive to the emotional baggage that our singers may be carrying. We must strive to bring love, acceptance, enthusiasm, confidence, passion, knowledge, preparation, and a desire to shape a creative hour in which students are challenged, in which they learn and accomplish something worthwhile, and in which youth connect with beauty, one another, and God. Directors must work to never bring their insecurities, anger, frustration, personal problems, and other negative attributes into the rehearsal room.

Common Vocal Problems

1. Matching Pitch

Work in private sessions with the youth who have problems matching pitch. Find where their speaking voice lies and where they can match pitch. Vocalize upward from that point. Use images like "reaching up to tap a bell" to reach higher notes. Have them sing easy songs they know (such as "My Country 'Tis of Thee" or "Kum Ba Yah") in their speaking voice range, then vocalize up using these songs. As students learn what it feels like to use their singing voice properly, pitch matching problems can usually be solved in three or four individual sessions.

2. Flatness

Singing flat is usually the result of lack of energy, or oversinging; thirds of a chord are also a common source of flatness. Think energy, think uniform vowels, think open space (open mouth as if surprised), and be sure that the tessitura is not too high for a particular singer.

3. Lack of Energy

Lack of energy in the choral sound can often be addressed with improved posture (hold your arms above your head, and bring them down slowly to achieve proper singing posture), connecting a physical activity to singing (such as clapping or moving your arms to reflect a phrase), and encouraging the choir by saying "on a one to ten scale, you just sang at a three. I'd like you to now sing that at a five; now at a seven; now at a ten."

Many choral problems in a youth choir can disappear when everyone in the choir confidently knows the notes, when the choir sings from memory, and when the conductor directs without being a slave to the score; that is, looking at the choir, showing energy and passion, and giving clear cues for entrances, cut-offs, dynamics, vowels, and consonants.

Warm-Up Exercises

Warm-ups serve different purposes at different times. Warm-ups separate us from the day, physically prepare the body to sing, as well as teach vocal technique, ear training, and rhythm. For a youth choir, if you are meeting at 8:00 A.M. on Sunday so that the choir can sing at an 8:30 service, physical and vocal warm-ups are the priority. At this early hour, consider including several physical warm-ups using hands and feet, and a brief time for the singers to massage the shoulders of the persons on both sides of them. If you are meeting at 5:00 P.M. on Sunday for a rehearsal, warm-ups that focus on intonation and blend may be the most important. Warm-ups ideally include both familiar and new material. There is a list of suggested warm-up resources in the Resources list on page 135.

Generally, a brief time of warm-ups might include the following:
- Stretching
- Singing posture exercise
- Humming and warming up the voice
- Tuning and pitch exercises (directly related to listening)
- Vowel work

Working with the Male Changing Voice

Working with the male "changing" voice is often a challenge for the church youth choir director. Several common methods of working with the male changing voice include:

1. Automatically place the singer in the bass or tenor section and let him do the best that he can until his voice has settled.
2. Use "cambiata" repertoire. The term *cambiata* (from the Latin "to change") refers to the voice of an adolescent male as it changes to its adult register.
3. Have all boys sing baritone on SAB literature.
4. Keep the "changing" guys singing as high as possible with the altos or sopranos.

A number of professional studies have offered several theories for the best way to work with the changing voice. The most famous of these is the "cambiata concept," developed in various ways by Irving Cooper, Don Collins, and John Cooksey; their work suggests the changing voice goes through four stages (Cooper and Collins) or six stages (Cooksey), from unchanged to "emerging adult voice." The alto/tenor approach of Duncan McKenzie suggests that the vocal change in boys is very gradual, moving from soprano to alto to tenor and possibly to bass over several years. The baritone/bass approach of Frederick Swanson states that the change may be very quick, even in the course of a few weeks. The voice pivoting approach of Sally Herman may be the most useful to church musicians; this method suggests keeping boys within their most comfortable range by pivoting them to other voice parts as needed.

In the church youth choir, we need to approach the changing voice through both music *and* social "eyes," for the sake of the spiritual element. Boys whose voices are changing need to feel that "it's no big deal," or we risk losing them from the choir. *Participation* in choir trumps everything. Four suggestions:

1. Work to create an atmosphere where boys of all ages are comfortable with the changing voice concept in their "head" voice. Vocalize out of the head voice. Occasionally, have a few of the older boys sing with the altos or sopranos on an anthem. Make it "cool" to sing in your head voice!
2. Move the changing voices ("super tenors") around—sometimes singing with the tenors, sometimes with the altos, or

even on a soprano melody. In fact, occasionally move individuals and groups around so that everyone is comfortable in more than one vocal place.

3. Use literature that guys with settled and changing voices enjoy singing. "Didn't My Lord Deliver Daniel" is an SAB arrangement that boys of all ages love to sing; even though the baritone part lies "high," all the boys can sing it, and love it. "Praise the Lord" has a tenor part that works great for changing voices. "Go Into the World" is a three-part anthem with parts labeled 1, 2, and 3; experiment with different sections or combinations on different parts.[5]

| unchanged | mid-voice I | mid-voice II | Mid-voice IIa | new baritone | settling baritone |

Changing Voices

The challenge to this approach is the need to know the individual voices, to be creative and energetic about the way that we work with voice placement and literature, and to create an accepting and open environment in the choir.

Female Voices

In recent years, Lynn Gackle and others have presented theories on the changing female voice. Gackle suggests that there are four stages of development for females, from child to young adult female; the two middle stages of development are directly related to body changes and often include breathiness, difficulty in achieving volume, and even hoarseness.[6]

Many vocal teachers suggest that teenage female voices should

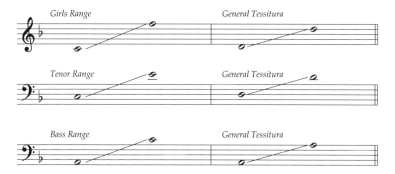

Vocal Ranges for Changed Voices

sing both soprano and alto. Like the boys, vocalize from high to low. Some experts advocate simply dividing the girls into group 1 and group 2, being sure to assign an equal number of strong singers and music readers to each group; on some anthems group 1 sings the soprano part, and on other anthems group 2 sings the soprano part.

In the church setting, it may be most helpful to divide the females into sopranos and altos, using the approach of two equal sections, but also being aware of older girls in the choir who can "anchor" the section because of the color or range of their voices.

With both boys and girls, it is helpful to have periodic one-on-one or small group voice check times. Make this a natural and easy part of choir life. The time before or after a rehearsal are great times to ask a few singers to gather around the piano and listen to each other's voices. When youth are comfortable in the choir setting, with their director, and with themselves, they will often initiate this discussion with a simple "Can you listen to me? I think my voice is changing since you last heard me."

Order in the Rehearsal

At the beginning of the year, and for the first few rehearsals, consider presenting R–E–C as a code of conduct:

R—Respect for the church, for the adults, the other youth, the music, and God

E—Energy. Nothing great will happen without energy—energy given to learning, singing, listening.

C—Commitment to being on time for every rehearsal and performance; commitment to respect and energy, which leads to passion.

In addition to R–E–C as our code of conduct, consider these additional suggestions for creating "energetic order" in youth choir rehearsals:

1. The rehearsal room must be conducive to singing. Be sure that the room looks ready for a rehearsal.

2. Have efficient systems for taking roll and for handling music.

3. Have a rehearsal plan that is displayed for the choir.

4. Keep singing as much as possible. Youth enjoy singing more than they enjoy listening.

5. Focus on contrasts in the order of music rehearsed: fast/slow; easy/difficult; familiar/new; success/challenge; stand/sit; loud/quiet.

6. Make use of sectional rehearsals so that everyone is kept busy throughout the rehearsal.

7. Use hand signals when choir members begin talking, for example, hold up a hand and "count down" with your fingers: 4-3-2-1.

8. Meet with each youth choir member one-on-one at the beginning of the year. Learn about their hopes, struggles, family, and spiritual beliefs. Share with them about yourself and about your dreams for the choir. Knowing one another will help with the respect factor in rehearsals.

9. Have a worship time at the beginning of the year in which each youth signs a covenant to pledge his or her attendance and good behavior.

.

Youth Choir Information Form

Name: _____ Name you go by: _____

Birthdate: _____ Grade: _____

Parent(s) Name(s): _____

Address: _____

Home Phone: _____ Cell Phone: _____

Email Address: _____

How often do you check your e-mail? _____

School you attend: _____

What school activities are you involved in? _____

_____

Instruments you play: _____

Do you have a job? _____

How many hours per week do you work? _____

Hobbies/Interests: _____

Favorite type of music: _____

Favorite thing to do in your free time:_____

Dream for our youth choir: _____

Prayer concerns: _____

_____

_____

Is there anything that it would help me to know about you?

_____

_____

_____

To be completed by the director:

Date of voice check: _____

Vocal range: _____ Tessitura: _____

Assigned voice part: _____ Tonal qualities: _____

Comments: _____

_____

_____

Notes

1. Blaine Lee, *The Power Principle: Influence with Honor* (New York: Fireside, 1998), p. 63.

2. Donald Neuen, *Choral Concepts: A Text for Conductors* (Belmont, CA: Wadsworth/Thomson Learning, 2002), p. 3.

3. Ibid., p. 13.

4. Ibid., p. 31.

5. "Didn't My Lord Deliver Daniel," traditional spiritual, arranged by Roger Emerson (Jenson), SAB; "Praise the Lord," traditional Cameroon, arranged by Ralph Johnson, (Earthsongs), SATB, percussion, catalog no. S-45; "Go Into the World," by Natalie Sleeth, (Choristers Guild), SAB or SSA or two-part (SA or mixed), keyboard, optional C instrument, catalog no. CGA209.

6. David Fiddle, "Changing Bodies, Changing Voices," *The Choral Journal*, December 2005.

CHAPTER SIX

PRAYERS IN REHEARSALS

Almighty God, at whose right hand are pleasures for evermore: We pray that as redeemed and forgiven children we may evermore rejoice in singing Thy praises. Grant, we beseech thee, that what we sing with our lips we may believe in our hearts, and what we believe in our hearts we may practice in our lives; so that being doers of the Word and not hearers only, we may obtain everlasting life; through Jesus Christ our Lord. Amen.

—Traditional Anglican prayer

Closing each rehearsal with a time of prayer builds community, reminds us of our greater purpose as a church choir, and connects persons with God. Here are some options:

1. Use a memorized prayer such as The Lord's Prayer, or the Prayer of Saint Francis, said in unison by the choir at the beginning or end of the rehearsal.

2. Allow time for prayer requests to be shared, followed by a prayer said by the director or student leader.

3. Use a prayer book. As students come into rehearsal they write joys and concerns on the page provided. These joys and concerns are then read out loud at the prayer time and a prayer is said. This method provides a written record, which can be emailed to everyone, and it cuts down on the time since you do

not take time for persons to voice their concerns. This method provides a means for people who don't feel comfortable speaking out loud to have their concerns and joys heard.

4. Create a Prayer Box. Students write their concerns on small pieces of paper provided and place them in the box.

5. Depending on the size of the group, go around the circle as each person says a "pow" or "wow" or passes; a prayer is said to close.

6. Divide into small groups (these groups could remain the same all semester/year or could change each week). Share prayer concerns followed by prayer.

7. To create a prayerful atmosphere, begin prayer time by singing a chorus or a Taizé song and then humming. Dim the lights. Light a candle.

8. Depending on the time available, use the sanctuary. Lights are dimmed; students can pray in the pews or go to the altar. After everyone has finished, join hands in a circle and close with a prayer.

9. Have a physical connection by joining hands for the closing prayer.

10. E-mail prayer concerns to the choir during the week.

HEART SONGS

REPERTOIRE

On your feet now—applaud God! . . .
Sing yourselves into his presence.
　　　　　　　　　　—Psalm 100:1-2 *(Message)*

"I loved singing every Sunday and I think it was those songs that kept
me from totally abandoning God."
　　　　　　　—Letter from a former youth choir member

Passionate singing by a youth choir happens when the singers own the anthem—that is, when the music and the text have become a "heart song" for each singer in the choir. A heart song is a song in which we find meaning, motivation, connection, and peace in our lives. A heart-song is the beautiful combination of choral excellence and emotional and spiritual connection.

Allison

A few years ago, Allison, who grew up singing in youth choir, went on a rappelling trip with a group of other college students. During her high-school years, Allison had sung in our youth choirs and had been a part of retreats, tours, and singing each

Sunday. Something went wrong on the rappelling trip, however, and suddenly Allison was suspended from the side of a mountain. Her fellow students could not rescue her, and Allison was forced to hang in the rappelling harness for over two hours while she waited for a helicopter to come to her rescue. To stay calm during this time, she sang songs that she had sung in youth choir, particularly, she told me, the anthem "Wings of the Dawn." This wonderful music is based on Psalm 139 and was a fantastic heart song for Allison during a very scary time.

Selecting Music

Selecting appropriate and compelling music for the choir is one of the choral director's most important activities. Marva Dawn says that the music of the church ultimately has to do with formation of the believer's character and formation of Christian community. Shallow music, she says, forms shallow people.[1] With that high calling in mind, consider the following seven evaluating questions as you choose youth choir repertoire:

1. Is the text worthwhile? (Is it theologically sound; does it hold spiritual insights?)
2. Does the anthem unify the faith community?
3. Is the anthem within the bounds of propriety for our faith community?
4. Does the anthem draw persons to the text and to a sense of a spiritual presence?
5. Is it musically strong (not trite)?
6. Does it expand our faith horizons?
7. Is it singable by my choir?

Variety is important, especially in youth choirs. Each year, consider singing at least one anthem from as many of these categories as is possible:

1. Renaissance
2. Baroque
3. Classical
4. Romantic

5. Modern
6. Chorales
7. Historic texts
8. Songs for men only, women only
9. Spirituals
10. Contemporary youth music
11. Global music
12. Choral arrangements of Contemporary Christian (CCM) songs or praise songs.

In every choir a choral standard is established over a period of time. Over the years, young people develop within themselves a standard for how their youth choir should sound and for what is appropriate for worship in the church. Often, they can more easily hear the voice of God through music that is unique to the church. But youth choir directors must also be open to the reality that young people naturally enjoy many styles of music. Consider including a "band" accompaniment on some anthems, or using a string quartet or brass ensemble for anthems in which these instruments are most appropriate.

Dance and Signing

Consider adding visual energy to the youth choir's music by including signing or liturgical dance as part of the presentation. Several books on signing are available, or consider asking a hearing impaired person in your community to teach the youth who will be signing. My preference is usually that the signing be done by a small group, not by the entire choir. Several anthems that lend themselves to signing include "Make Me an Instrument of Thy Peace," "Jacob's Ladder," and "Prayer of the Children."[2] "Make Me an Instrument of Thy Peace" is especially effective with several girls signing the women's choral part and several guys signing the men's choral part. "Jacob's Ladder" is very effective when signed only by a group of guys, and "Prayer of the Children" is most effective when signed by one person.

Liturgical dances can be conceived by persons in your church who are dancers. The dancers should wear long skirts and tops that do not draw attention to the body. Liturgical dance is, in some ways, a gentle mixture of dance and mime. At its best, liturgical dance feels appropriate to worship, and helps viewers to be drawn into the words and music of the anthem. We are a visual society, and dance can be a very effective way of conveying the message of the text. Youth choir anthems that lend themselves to dance include "Weave Me," "Climb to the Top of the Highest Mountain," and "Thy Will Be Done."[3]

Smaller Choirs

Many youth choirs consist of seven girls and two guys, or a similar mix of vocal parts. These choirs can thrive if the directors are creative. Consider adapting SATB literature by singing it in unison, by alternating unison boys and unison girls, by singing some of the anthem in two parts, or by singing three or four parts at cadences and concluding measures. Canons work very well for small groups, and denominational songbooks, such as *The Faith We Sing* offer a wealth of possible literature.[4] Consider the following repertoire for small groups from *The Faith We Sing* (the Singer's Edition is the most helpful for ensemble singing):

- Arise, Shine
- Great Is the Lord
- How Majestic Is Your Name
- As the Dear
- Halle, Halle, Halle
- Praise, Praise, Praise the Lord

Additional anthem literature from various publishers that can be easily adapted to one to three parts:

- Go Into the World
- Cantate Domino
- Ride the Chariot
- Sing to the Lord a Joyful Song
- Walk in the Light[5]

The list of possible repertoire for small youth choirs is limitless. In addition to the selections already listed, much of the literature in the three repertoire lists that conclude this chapter are adaptable to creative arranging, particularly the anthems in the two-part and three-part lists. I have indicated the anthems that might be most successfully adapted for small choirs with an asterisk.

Youth Choir Repertoire by Music Periods

1. Renaissance
- CALL TO REMEMBRANCE — Richard Farrant (Belwin, 64061)
- I HAVE LONGED FOR THY SAVING HEALTH — William Byrd (Gray, 01679)
- LO, HOW A ROSE — Michael Praetorius (E. C. Schirmer, 2290)
- LORD FOR THY TENDER MERCIES' SAKE — Richard Farrant (E. C. Schirmer, 55374)
- COME YE SERVANTS OF THE LORD — Christopher Tye (Hinshaw, 508)
- PSALLITE — Michael Praetorius (Mercury, 167)
- RUN YOU SHEPHERDS — Thomas Morley (Hope, 1692)
- *WE WILL PRAISE YOU — William Praetorius (Choristers Guild, 350) (three-part canon)

2. Baroque
- ALLELUIA, from Cantata 142 — J. S. Bach (Galazy, 1.2729)
- BLEST ARE THEY WHOSE SPIRITS LONG — G. F. Handel/Hal H. Hopson (Choristers Guild, CGA183)
- GLORIA — A. Vivaldi (Walton, 2043)
- GLORY IN THE NAME OF GOD — G. F. Handel (Abingdon Press, 024986)
- HALLELUJAH, AMEN — G. F. Handel (Alfred, 7740)
- YOU ARE MY LIGHT AND MY SALVATION — G. F. Handel (Abingdon Press, 0687497299)
- SING A NEW SONG — H. Schütz/Carolyn Jennings (Belwin, 7601)

- SOUND THE TRUMPET — H. Purcell/Hal H. Hopson (Fischer, 8056)
- *WITH SONGS OF REJOICING — J. S. Bach/Hal H. Hopson (Fischer, S086) (two parts)

3. **Classical**
   - GLORIA *(Heiligmesse)* — F. J. Haydn (Walton, 2031)
   - GOD IS OUR REFUGE AND STRENGTH — W. A. Mozart (Chantry, 6712)
   - *HALLELUJAH ROUND OF PRAISE — W. A. Mozart (Choristers Guild, 423) (three part canon)
   - HOW LOVELY ARE THE MESSENGERS — F. Mendelssohn (Choristers Guild, 501)
   - OH, WHAT BEAUTY, LORD, APPEARS — W. A. Mozart (Choristers Guild, 666)
   - PRAISE WE SING TO THEE — F. J. Haydn/Morten Luvaas (Kjos, 2015)

4. **Romantic**
   - CANTIQUE — G. Fauré/John Rutter (Hinshaw 933)
   - MASS in G — F. Schubert (Schirmer)
   - MESSE BASSE — G. Fauré (Presser 312-40598)
   - HOW BLESSED — A. Bruckner (Choral Art 154)
   - JESUS, GRANT ME HOPE AND COMFORT — C. Franck (Schmitt 1544)
   - STRIKE THE CYMBAL — F. Schubert (Choristers Guild 684)

5. **Modern**
   - BEST OF ALL FRIENDS — K. Lee Scott (Morning Star 50-9003)
   - CAROL OF THE BELLS — M. Leontovich (Fischer 4604)
   - *FOR THE BEAUTY OF THE EARTH — John Rutter (Hinshaw) (four-part and two-part versions are available).
   - THE GLORY OF THE FATHER — Egil Hovland (Walton 2973)
   - LOOK AT THE WORLD — John Rutter (Hinshaw)

6. Chorales (from standard denominational hymnals)
- CHRIST, WHOSE GLORY FILLS THE SKIES
- FAIREST LORD JESUS
- IF YOU BUT TRUST (SUFFER) GOD TO GUIDE YOU
- LET THE WHOLE CREATION CRY
- THE LORD IS MY SHEPHERD

7. Historic Texts
- CANTATE DOMINO — G. Pitoni (Bourne, 55)
- FESTIVAL SANCTUS — John Leavitt (Belwin, 8821)
- GLORIA IN EXCELSIS — John Leavitt (Belwin, 9116)
- HODIE CHRISTUS NATUS EST — Sherri Porterfield (Belwin, 9043)
- KYRIE — John Leavitt (Belwin, 8904)
- SANCTUS — Sherri Porterfield (Alfred, 7870)
- *A JUBILANT SONG — Mary Lynn Lightfoot (Sacred Music Press, 10/1026) (two parts)

8. Songs for Men and Women
Men
- EZEKIEL SAW THE WHEEL — Donald E. Large (Kjos. 5528-7)
- MARY HAD A BABY — Robert Shaw (Schirmer. 10191)
- PRAYER OF THE CHILDREN — Kent Bestor (Flammer)
- STEAL AWAY — B. W. Dennard (Shawnee 279)

Women
- GO WHERE I SEND THEE — Paul Caldwell (Earthsongs)
- LOVE CAME DOWN AT CHRISTMAS — Dede Duson (Kjos, 6184)
- PSALM 67 — Julie Knowles (Jenson, 41716013)
- PSALM 100 — Rene Clausen (Mark Foster, 917)

9. Spirituals
- DOWN BY THE RIVERSIDE — John Rutter (Oxford, 84.248)

- HUSH! SOMEBODY'S CALLIN' MY NAME — B. W. Dennard (Shawnee, 1802)
- *I AM HIS CHILD — Moses Hogan (Alliance)
- KUMBAYA — Paul Sjolund (Hinshaw, 617)
- MY GOD IS SO HIGH — Moses Hogan (Alliance)
- *WALK IN THE LIGHT — Andre Thomas (Choristers Guild, CGA1063)
- SHUT DE DO — Randy Stonehill (Chancel, 301026167)
- PRAISE HIS HOLY NAME — Keith Hampton (Earthsongs)
- TRUE LIGHT — Keith Hampton (Earthsongs)
- CITY CALLED HEAVEN — Josephine Poelinitz (Plymouth)

10. Youth Music – Contemporary
- BE NOT AFRAID — Taylor Davis (Choristers Guild, CGA991)
- WEAVE ME, LORD — Linda Spencer (GlorySound)
- FOR ALL THAT IS — Taylor Davis (Choristers Guild, CGA1037)
- LORD, MAKE ME AN INSTRUMENT OF THY PEACE — Jody Lindh (Choristers Guild, CGA612)
- MANY GIFTS, ONE SPIRIT — Allen Pote (Coronet, 392-41388)
- *PRAISE HIS HOLY NAME — Keith Hampton (Earthsongs)
- *PSALM 139 — Allen Pote (Choristers Guild, 610)
- WINGS OF THE DAWN — Linda Spencer (Glory Sound, 6183)

11. Global Music
- Songs from Taizé — Jacques Berthier (GIA, various hymnals)
- FREEDOM IS COMING — South African (Walton)
- FOUR AFRICAN HYMNS —J. Nathan Corbitt (Choristers Guild, CGA686)
- *HALLE, HALLE, HALLE — arr. Marty Haugen (GIA, G-3961)
- O SIFUNI MUNGU — arr. David Maddux (Word, 3010456168)
- PRAISE THE LORD —Cameroon/arr. Ralph Johnson (Earthsongs)

12. Contemporary Christian songs or praise songs

Arrangements are available each year from several publishers and you will find downloadable contemporary Christian music on many websites. You will need to arrange them carefully for your choir, considering range and number of singer.

Two-Part Youth Choir Anthems
- A LENTEN WALK — Hal H. Hopson (Augsburg, 11-10568)
- ALABARE — arr. Ronald Nelson (ASMI 658)
- COME, THOU FOUNT OF EVERY BLESSING — Hal H. Hopson (Harold Flammer, EA 5021)
- HEAR MY WORDS — Stephen Paulus (Hinshaw, HMC-201)
- I WANT JESUS TO WALK WITH ME — Hal H. Hopson (Choristers Guild, CGA-701)
- KEEP ME FAITHFULLY IN THY PATHS — G. F. Handel/Richard Proulx (GIA, G 2355)
- LET ALL THE WORLD IN EVERY CORNER SING — Jody Lindh (Choristers Guild, CGA-573)
- MAY THE PEACE OF THE LORD — Douglas E. Wagner (Hope, A-606)
- COME AND MOURN — Hal H. Hopson (Hope, HH 3907)
- WALK IN THE LIGHT — Andre Thomas (Choristers Guild)

Three-Part Youth Choir Anthems
- ALLELUIA ROUND — William Boyce/Richard/Proulx (GIA, G-2494)
- BE NOT AFRAID — Douglas Wagner (Hope, A683)•
  CANTATE DOMINO — Anna Laura Page (Alfred, 11416)
- CHRIST THE LORD IS RISEN TODAY — Johnson (Word, 301 0626 169)
- FOREVER BLEST IS HE — G. F. Handel/R. Stanton (Flammer D-5241)

- GLORIA IN EXCELSIS DEO — Dave and Jean Perry (Shawnee, D-325)
- HALLELUJAH ROUND OF PRAISE — W. A. Mozart/Austin C. Lovelace (Choristers Guild, CGA-423)
- KYRIE ELEISON — Andrea Klouse (Hal Leonard, 08704233)
- PRAISE AGAIN AND AGAIN — Michael Barrett (Gloria Sound, D-5440)
- STRIKE THE CYMBAL — F. Schubert/Austin C. Lovelace (Choristers Guild, CGA 684)

Notes

1. Marva Dawn, *Reaching Out Without Dumbing Down: A Theology of Worship for This Urgent Time* (Grand Rapids: Wm. B. Eerdmans, 1995), p. 13.

2. "Make Me an Instrument of Thy Peace" by Jody Lindh (Choristers Guild); "Jacob's Ladder" by Daniel Kallman (Morningstar); and "Prayer of the Children" by Kent Bestor (Warner Brothers).

3. "Weave Me" by Linda Spencer (Glory Sound); "Climb to the Top of the Highest Mountain" by Carolyn Jennings (Kjos); and "Thy Will Be Done" by Craig Courtney (Beckenhorst).

4. Hoyt L. Hickman, ed., *The Faith We Sing* (Nashville: Abingdon Press, 2000).

5. "Go Into the World," by Natalie Sleeth, SAB or SSA or two-part (SA or mixed), keyboard, optional C instrument, catalog no. CGA-209 (Choristers Guild); "Cantate Domino" by Anna Laura Page (Alfred), no. 11416; "Ride the Chariot" by Patsy Simms (Theodore Presser), no. 392-41866; "Sing to the Lord a Joyful Song" by Hal H. Hopson (Flammer), no. FA-5001; "Walk in the Light," arranged by Andre Thomas (Choristers Guild), catalog no. CGA-1062.

THE POWER OF RETREATS AND TOURS

CHAPTER EIGHT

RETREATS

Purity of heart allows us to see more clearly,
not only our own needy, distorted, and anxious self,
but also the caring face of our compassionate God.
When that vision remains clear and sharp,
it will be possible to move into the midst
of a tumultuous world with a heart at rest.[1]
—Henri Nouwen, *The Way of the Heart*

A meaningful and memorable retreat doesn't happen without careful planning and commitment. A youth choir retreat that will become a great experience for your choir members should include:

- Great musical experiences (great music, great rehearsals)
- Great worship experiences that help youth reconnect with God (see chapter 10)
- An activity through which each youth is affirmed
- Activities that help youth connect in a deep way with other youth (such as small groups)
- Something unexpected (such as a gift, a dance, a special dinner)

Suggestions for a Great Retreat

1. Learning great music is the core of a good choir retreat. Have some anthems that can be completely learned on retreat, as well as some that are very challenging.

2. Choose your camp carefully. Ideally, it should be no farther than ninety minutes away, be a place that is conducive to rehearsals, worship, and games, and be youth friendly.

3. Do not show movies unless they are shown for a reason. Retreats should pull us away from TV/entertainment. Focus on one another, God, and the choir's mission.

4. Youth should return home relaxed and *rested*. Allow time for youth to get eight hours of sleep. So many young people have such hectic schedules that they rarely get a good night's sleep.

5. Free time is an important part of retreats for older youth. Try to give a block of at least two and a half hours one afternoon and one hour at the end of the day for unstructured free time. Retreats for 7th to 9th graders, however, should include much less free time.

6. Good food, appropriate for teenagers, is essential.

7. Use student leaders and the youth pastor in leadership.

8. Include both organized sports and options for "pick-up" games for those members of the group that enjoy athletics.

9. Both small and large youth choirs may benefit by joining together with another choir for a retreat.

Ideas for Group Building and Surprises

- A dance (loud and fun)
- A theme dinner (with decorations)
- Skits (keep it clean)
- Bag skits. Provide a bag with an assortment of unrelated items for each group. The groups are then given fifteen minutes to prepare a skit in which every item in the bag is used and every member of their group has a speaking part.
- Awards (most creative, most enthusiastic, and so on)
- Retreats with a theme (using a phrase from a song, such as "Many Gifts, One Spirit")
- Choir Olympics (potato bag races, hamburger-eating contest, pass-the-egg with spoons, and others). Use your small groups as teams.

- Guest speaker
- Concert by a favorite local band or artist. Ask the band members or artist to share their faith story as a part of the concert.
- Talent show
- Make or gather small gifts to give to persons at nursing homes where you sing.
- Drawings. Have drawings for prizes at the beginning or end of rehearsal times.
- Have a mini-concert for parents when you arrive home.

Affirmations

CARE BAGS

Have sandwich-size paper bags, each with a youth's name on it, placed around a room. During the course of the retreat, let members of the choir put notes of care and love in the bags. Ask persons to not read the notes in their bag until an assigned time when everyone does this together in a worshipful setting.

BABY PICTURES

Have parents secretly send you a baby picture of each youth. The picture can be placed on the individual's care bag (described above), or the pictures can be placed on posters around the room.

GIFTS OF THE SPIRIT AFFIRMATION

Divide the choir into small groups of five to seven persons. Give each person a heavyweight piece of paper and ten computer address labels (the kind that are sticky on the back). Read Galatians 5:22, which lists the fruit of the Spirit. Invite each person to write to each person in their small group (using the computer labels), which fruit of the Spirit that they see in that person. Once everyone has written something for each person in their group, take time for each person in the group to be "it," at which time each person in the group presents their affirmation to that person.

Small Groups

Consider dividing the choir into small groups or "family" groups for sharing times during the retreat. Prepare several questions that help youth get to know one another and to share at a deep level.

Note

1. Henri Nouwen, *The Way of the Heart* (New York: HarperCollins, 1981), p. 90.

CHOIR RETREAT REGISTRATION
(Retreat is Friday through Sunday)

THIS FORM IS DUE ON SUNDAY, _____

NAME _____ PHONE _____
ADDRESS _____
CITY/ZIP _____
SCHOOL _____GRADE _____
BIRTHDATE _____
YOUR CELL PHONE NUMBER _____
MOTHER'S CELL PHONE _____
FATHER'S CELL PHONE _____
YOUR E-MAIL ADDRESS _____

VOICE PART (circle): Soprano Alto Tenor Bass

ROOMMATE SUGGESTIONS: Room assignments will be made so that everyone can get to know some new people. Please list two persons with whom you would like to room; they may or may not wind up in your room, however.
1. _____
2. _____

MEDICAL INFORMATION: Please list any information concerning medical or emotional problems that the adult leaders should be aware of, such as allergies, prescription medications, health problems, and so on.

EMERGENCY CONTACT PERSON/PHONE NUMBER IN CASE YOUR PARENTS CANNOT BE REACHED
_____

PARENT'S PERMISSION

With my signature, I give my consent, as parent/guardian of the above named youth, for emergency medical treatment in the event that I cannot be reached, and give my permission for this youth to ride on transportation provided by the church.

Parent Signature _____

Date _____

YOUTH COVENANT

I pledge to do my best to make this retreat a great experience, not only for myself but also for everyone else. I promise to obey the rules established by the youth and adult leaders, such as being on time and actively participating in events, staying in my room after curfew, obeying the "visiting" rules, and so on. I also promise that during the retreat I will not use and will not have in my possession smoking materials of any kind, any liquor, or any illegal drugs. More than not breaking any "rules," I pledge to try to have a positive attitude, to work hard at rehearsals, to participate in the worship, small-group, and fun events. I also realize that this is a church retreat and that the ultimate purpose is to help each of us to come away from the weekend feeling closer to God and to each other.

Youth signature _____

Date _____

Sample Schedule

RETREAT SCHEDULE

Friday
4:30 P.M.	Meet
5:00	Leave
6:30	Arrive
7:00	Dinner
7:30	Worship
8:00	Sectional/Group Work
9:45	Break
10:00	Worship
11:00	In Cabins

Saturday
8:30 A.M.	Breakfast
9:15	Worship
9:30	Sectional/Group Work
10:30	Small-Group Activity
11:00	Full Rehearsal
12:00 P.M.	Lunch
1:00	Full Rehearsal
2:00	Free Time
5:00	Rehearsal
6:00	Supper
7:00	Skits
8:30	Worship
9:30	Coffee House

Sunday
9:00 A.M.	Breakfast
9:45	Full Rehearsal
11:00	Worship/Sharing
12:00 P.M.	Lunch
1:15	Leave
3:00	Sing for parents at church

CHAPTER NINE

TOURS

*The Spirit of the Lord is on me, because he has anointed me to
preach good news to the poor. He has sent me to proclaim freedom
for the prisoners and recovery of sight for the blind.*

—Luke 4:18 (NIV)

*"For a solid week our choir lived a little piece of heaven on earth.
. . . I realize that something special happened for a reason,
and I cannot take that for granted."*

—Letter from a former youth choir member

Choir tour is, for most youth choir members, the culmination
of the choir year. The memory of the previous tour can pro-
pel the choir during the first half of the year, and anticipa-
tion of the next tour can energize the group during the second half
of the year. Choir tour should not be presented as a reward or "fun
trip"; rather, it should serve as an integral part of our ministry to
others, and an integral part of the goal of helping each young person in the choir to grow musically and in his/her faith journey.

Five Objectives

1. Minister to others through music and personal interaction.
2. Grow musically and spiritually from the intense rehearsal
and performance schedule.

3. Deepen the fellowship within the group, getting to know one another better, and developing deep and lasting friendships.

4. Experience and deepen our relationship with God through intentional times of worship.

5. Expand our understanding and appreciation for the diversity of the world by learning about other people, cities, churches, and cultures (to move us out of the "bubble" in which most of us live).

Ten Suggestions for Tours

1. Establish and enforce attendance requirements prior to tour.

2. Although the positive experiences of tours generally have nothing to do with where the tour travels, do plan a trip with a "hook" to energize the group.

3. Begin each day with devotions and other group activities, and also have a brief devotion and prayer time before each concert. Give youth opportunities to lead these times.

4. Give as many youth as possible a specific job to do. Give adult sponsors specific jobs.

5. Change roommate assignments each night, or at least once or twice during the tour so that youth have the opportunity to make new friends.

6. Have all youth sign a covenant before leaving.

7. Assemble a tour booklet that includes a daily schedule, a list of guidelines, a list of things to bring, and other helpful information.

8. Choose adult sponsors carefully. Adults need to be liked and respected by youth, supportive of the director and his/her decisions, and willing to put the needs of the youth first. Try to assemble an adult group with some variety (young, older, parents, non-parents, couples, singles), allowing these adults to do as much as possible so that the director is free to work with the music and to be with the youth. Allow the other adults to do the things that the director does not do well.

9. Stick to the rules, including consequences when rules are broken.

10. Do everything you can to help the choir be prepared musically before tour; avoid having extended rehearsals during the tour unless absolutely needed.

Tour Choir/Church Choir

Young people ultimately usually see events and people as they really are. A choir whose primary objective is *touring* will not be as "successful" as a choir whose primary objective is *worship leadership*. The tour should be an outgrowth of worship leadership. If your choir does not sing weekly, do sing as often as possible in worship and in outreach situations.

Rehearsal Week

Establishing the tradition of a "rehearsal week" can greatly enhance the effectiveness of a tour. Rehearse each night of the three to five days before the summer tour. Put a high priority on the importance of everyone being present for this week. Plan for each night to have a special bonus, such as singing at the homeless mission, giving tour T-shirts, or having a swim party after the rehearsal—the possibilities are limitless!

Concert Venues

Consider the following as possible venues for tour concerts: churches, retirement homes, nursing homes, prisons, camps and facilities for special needs children, homeless shelters, and hospitals. It seems to me that one of our goals for tour must be to expose youth to the hurting people of the world, and to move them beyond their comfort zone.

In an essay for his college English class, David, a former member of the choir, wrote:

The concert began and I found the words spilling from my mouth as if out of habit rather than a conscious process. Instead of focusing on what I was doing, I was able to concentrate more on the awe-inspiring audience as they rocked back and forth in their wheel chairs and exclaimed indistinguishable words of joy. As one of my friends stepped out for his solo, I saw the differences between a person with a handicap and a "normal" person are really not all that different. The loving tears that flowed from his eyes and that trickled from the woman in the audience were the same tears that swelled in my eyes. Singing to these residents helped me to realize that we humans are all so similar, some just have gifts others were not so lucky to receive.

Consider at least one concert for each day of the trip. In other words, if the tour is eight days, try to present a total of eight concerts; some days may include two concerts so that a full day can be kept free for special events.

Many choirs also have had the fun of singing the National Anthem at a major league baseball game. Contact with these teams must be made very early in the tour planning process.

Day or Overnight Tours

A tour does not have to be an entire week! Consider a one-day or overnight tour either locally or staying within an hour or two of home. In this time of very busy teenagers and the high cost of transportation and lodging, it might, in many situations, be more effective to begin a tradition of a weekend tour or of several one-day tours rather than the usual week-long trip. The same principles apply—do several concerts, do something fun, do something that affirms each youth, and conclude the day with meaningful worship.

Tours and Mission Trips

Some churches have found that combining a mission component to the choir tour is the most effective way of experiencing a choir trip. Some tours go to one city, stay in a college dorm, and spend their day doing backyard Bible schools, or working on a work project such as repairing houses, and then presenting several concerts in the evenings of the week.

Joining with Another Choir

Smaller youth choirs may want to consider joining with another youth choir for tour. This can be a great experience, and give everyone the opportunity to be a part of a larger, and perhaps stronger, choir.

Youth Cue Events

Youth Cue is a nondenominational organization that offers many resources for church youth choirs. One of the most popular events are the events that draw several hundred teenagers for two days of rehearsals and a closing concert with orchestra. Many youth choirs find these events to be a great alternative to the traditional tour. Additional information can be had at www.youth-choirs.org.

Visiting Spiritual Places on Tour

Two of the most meaningful spiritual places to visit are a monastery and a beautiful Gothic cathedral. The youth choirs at Brentwood visited St. Meinrad monastery in Indiana many times, and always found the spirit of prayer to be an infectious experience for the members of the choir. Listening to a monk talk about his spiritual life, asking the monk questions, and having time for personal and corporate worship are highlights of the visit. It is, as one youth told me, a "cleansing experience." Another powerful experience is visiting a large Gothic cathedral, particularly places such as the St. Louis Cathedral and Washington National

Cathedral. The beauty and awe of these buildings always resonate with youth, and provide a meaningful experience. Beautiful places in the outdoors are also powerful places in which to connect with the spirit of God.

Megan wrote this about the choir's visit to the St. Louis Cathedral:

> As we filed in, none of us even dared to breathe. The silence could almost be weighed in pounds, but it was the sheer holiness of it all that astounded us. But more important than the marble floors and the tall wax candles, we knew that God was indeed surrounding each and every one of us as we worshipped.

Ideas for Enhancing the Tour Experience

GIFT BAGS

Consider having members of the congregation make a gift bag for one (or more) of the tour participants. Each person is assigned (or chooses) a choir member to sponsor and is given a copy of the form on the next page. Bags should be due seven days before departure.

During tour week, give everyone on the trip time to write a letter of thanks to the person who made his or her bag. Have the envelopes pre-addressed and pre-stamped. A guidelines sheet is given to each person for assistance in writing the thank-you note.

This project is wonderful not only for the youth who receives the bags, but also for the adults who make the bags. This project allows everyone, young and old, to be a part of tour, and receiving a personal letter from a youth on tour is very meaningful for those who have made a bag.

Consider providing the actual bag that persons will use so that every youth receives the same size bag.

This information is given to each person who signs up to make a gift bag.

GUIDELINES FOR CHOIR-TOUR GIFT BAGS

Your Choir Member: _____

Thank you for being a part of the choir-tour ministry by making this Gift Bag.

1. Gift bags should be no larger than approximately 8" x 10".
2. Bags may include a small amount of candy, gum, snacks, magazines or other appropriate material.
3. Most important of all, your bag should include a letter from you. Tell about yourself and tell your young person that you will be praying for him/her during choir-tour week. Please also share a favorite Scripture and why it is important to you.
4. The name of the person for whom the bag is made must be prominently displayed on the front of the bag.
5. Bags must be turned in no later than (*insert date here*).

****

Please complete the following form, tear it off, and leave it in the designated box <u>when you get your name</u>. Please print clearly.

Youth for whom the bag is being made: _____

Person making the bag: _____

Name _____

Mailing address _____

City _____ State _____ Zip_____

The following instructions are given to each youth on choir tour when they have the opportunity to write a thank-you letter to the person who made their gift bag.

GUIDELINES FOR WRITING LETTERS TO THE PERSON WHO MADE YOUR GIFT BAG

1. Address your letter: "Dear Mr." or "Dear Mr. and Mrs. . . ."
2. Thank them for the bag.
3. Tell them what you liked.
4. Tell them about yourself—your grade in school, what you like to do, and so on.
5. Tell them about what's been fun or meaningful about choir tour.
6. Invite them to Home Concert. Ask them to bring their friends and neighbors with them. It's going to be a great concert!
7. Sign your letter, place it in the pre-addressed envelope, and seal the envelope.

Each group leader should collect all the letters for the group.

LETTER TO YOURSELF

Write a letter to yourself telling about your experiences on the retreat or tour, commitments you want to make to God, to yourself, and to the group. Seal the letter in an envelope addressed to yourself. These letters are collected and mailed two weeks after the event. This reminds each youth of his/her commitments and helps keep the spirit of the event living on.

JOURNAL

Each youth is invited to keep a journal during the retreat or tour. A journal might be provided with questions related to each day:

- My favorite moment today was
- I got to know _____ better today.
- The best part of our concert today was
- I saw God at work today through

TOUR BOOKS

Many directors publish a tour booklet for each participant in the tour. Included in this booklet are the detailed itinerary and daily schedules, rules for the trip, job assignments, contact numbers, devotional thoughts, and a list of what to bring (and what not to bring).

STORYTELLING

Sharing stories with each other is an important group and spirit builder. We might also call this exercise "processing." Either immediately after a concert, or in our group and worship time at the end of the day, ask members of the choir to share what they saw, felt, and experienced. Focus the group on thinking about looking for ways in which they saw God at work in the concert.

FAMILY GROUPS

Family groups can be done on a retreat or tour, or as a part of the entire choir year. Divide the entire group into small groups of about seven persons. Ideally, have an adult as part of each group. The family group's goal is to get to know persons whom they do not already know. Assign questions for the groups to discuss, or have each person in the small groups share a POW! (a bad thing) and a WOW! (a good thing) that happened to them this past week. Have each group share prayer concerns.

SCRIPTURE STUDY

Pick a scripture or parable for each day on tour or retreat. Provide background on the meaning and context of the scripture. Allow youth to share what the scripture means to them. Consider memorizing a theme verse for the week, or memorizing a daily theme verse.

SECRET PALS

Assign each retreat or tour participant a "secret pal." During the course of the retreat or tour, assign special things to be done for the pal, such as:
- A gift not costing over $1.00
- A note with your favorite Bible verse
- A creative card made from magazines and glue
- A letter

At the end of the event, have a time when names of secret pals are shared.

PRAYER PARTNERS

Use the same ideas as secret pals, but make praying for the assigned person the focus.

GIVING OF CROSSES ON TOUR

Consider giving each member of the choir a cross at one of the worship services during tour. Our tradition has been to give a different cross "necklace" each year:
- "Jerusalem" cross (purchased from store)
- Nail cross (made by church member)
- Wooden cross (made by church member)

GIVING AWAY CROSSES AT CONCERTS

Inexpensive wood cross necklaces can be purchased in large quantities from on-line stores (like Oriental Trading Company).

At Brentwood, we purchased several hundred of these crosses and gave them away during tour concerts. Prior to singing one of our anthems, we told the audience that we would like to give them a gift of a cross and asked them to raise their hand if they would like to receive one. During the anthem, six to eight students left the choir and offered the crosses to those who had raised their hands.

CELEBRATION LUNCH

Consider having a celebration lunch or dinner for the members of the choir and their families a few days after returning home from tour. This event is a way of being sure that all parents have an opportunity to see and hear what happened on tour (in case they have a child who answered the question about what happened on tour with, "Oh, not much!").

At Brentwood, we invited each family to bring a large dish of food. After a quick lunch, we had a "slide show" with pictures of each day's events; several youth told the story of the week as we went through these pictures. Following this presentation, two or three youth told what the tour experience meant to them personally; I usually invited at least one or two youth who had had a particularly meaningful week to share. I then introduced the sponsors so that this did not have to be done at home concert. The final event was a "slide show" of the tour with carefully chosen music playing in the background.

The Celebration Lunch builds community within the group and among parents and helps everyone to see more clearly the "big picture" of how God has been a part of the ministry of choir tour. For younger brothers and sisters, it is another way of creating an "I can't wait to be in youth choir" attitude.

Choir Tour Sponsors

Having a great team of competent, mature, and cooperative adults is crucial to a great tour experience. I have found it most effective to include both adults who have previously been a part of tours and understand what needs to happen, as well as including adults who are new to the experience. Including two to four college students as sponsors can add tremendous energy to the tour experience. The youth minister should also be a part of the sponsor group, if possible.

Meet with the adults prior to tour and each day on tour. At a meeting prior to tour, consider giving each adult a complete roster, itinerary, and a list of youth with special medical conditions, allergies, and those who are taking medication. Consider the following suggestions for the adult sponsors:

- Remember that you are a guest on the choir's trip.
- Always be early.
- Be an encourager.
- Be sensitive to the feelings of the other adults.
- Problems and decisions ultimately are the director's responsibility.
- Support the rules, plans, other adults, and the director.
- Keep the director informed of all issues.
- Flexibility is your favorite word.
- No alcohol or smoking.
- Reach out to the youth who are sad, or are not connecting with other youth.

The following suggestions are given to college sponsors on the high-school trip, and to high-school seniors who are spon-sors on the junior-high trip.

FIFTEEN WAYS TO BE A LEADER
1. Positive behavior at rehearsals and all events
2. Be positive about EVERYTHING!
3. Work to make something go well, especially when it's NOT going well.
4. Reach out to people.
   - Be there for those who need a friend.
   - Speak to as many persons as possible.
   - Don't stay in your "clique."
5. Work at the job no one wants to do (like cleanup).
6. Be the first one at events.
7. Help *every time* to set up or take down or clean up.
8. Be the first one up in the morning; be the one that helps the cabin to go to bed.
9. If you are leading an event, work on it; practice it; do not *wing* it!
10. If you say you are going to do it, then do it; and do it better than anyone else would do it.
11. Do not allow anything negative to happen (don't let people break rules; don't look the other way).
12. If you give yourself to making tour a great experience for others, then people will respect you and you will end up feeling proud of yourself.
13. Real leaders lead *partly* by speaking and instructing others in what to do; they lead *mostly* by example. If you're consistently positive, on task, and working hard to make something work, others will eventually follow your lead.
14. Be a spiritual leader. Share your faith.
15. Get rest at night so that you can be at your best each day.

Ideas for Logistics

BUS BOOK

Each bus and van on tour should have a notebook that includes everything an adult or youth might need to know. Having this information helps everyone to know what's happening, gives a central source for information, and cuts down on questions for the director. Included in the book are the itinerary, list of those on the trip, concert program, maps, what to wear each day, and information about the cities and places to be visited each day.

WORSHIP

Worship is central to the choir tour experience. Begin or end every day with a devotion and reflection time and have extended evening worship times during the tour week (examples for worship events are found in chapter 10).

MEALS

Mall food courts are, of course, the best place to quickly feed a group of hungry teenagers. Purchasing sandwiches from Subway or other stores and having a picnic at a rest stop is also a great way to feed a large group.

LODGING

Many choirs still do some concerts in churches, after which youth are housed in homes of church members.

Many church youth choirs, however, are moving away from the "host homes" concept, in part due to safety concerns. Colleges used to be a great place to house choirs on tour; the costs of dorms, however, is now often higher than staying at a hotel. So most choirs now travel each day and stay in a hotel each night.

Here are some suggestions to help your check-in at a hotel to be quick and easy:

1. Make arrangements several months ahead.
2. Request that rooms be in blocks together.
3. Request a "conference" room for group and worship time.

4. Request that all charges be put on the master bill.

5. Send a rooming list at least ten days ahead.

6. Request that adults be put in rooms near the rooms of youth.

7. Send a set of envelopes—one for each room you are renting—on which you have already placed the names of the youth or adults who will be in that room. Number each envelope so that each group that is rooming together knows the number of the envelope that they need. Ask that the hotel put the proper keys in these envelopes. These envelopes should be ready when you walk in the door.

8. Ask that the hotel have a copy of the rooming list with the room numbers for each of your adult sponsors. This list should be ready when you walk in the door of the hotel.

9. Have the financial arrangements worked out prior to arrival.

10. Call the hotel a week before, the day before, and the day of arrival to verify that all of your requests have been addressed.

11. Have one youth per room responsible for getting the envelope with the keys and for distributing the keys to other persons in the room.

DIRECTIONS

Prepare a Master Itinerary with a detailed schedule for the trip, including names of hotels, performance venues, and other places that the choir will be visiting, contact persons and phone numbers for each of these places, and detailed travel directions for how to get to each place that you are going. Do not rely totally on directions obtained from the Internet; double-check correct directions with each of the places that you are going. Hours invested in correct directions prior to the trip will save leaders from frustration during the trip. Be sure that every bus, van, or car in your group has a copy of this Master Itinerary.

BUS CHECK-IN

If your choir is traveling on a chartered bus, or if you are using multiple vans, a system for quick and accurate roll call is needed.

Options might include:
1. Have a list of everyone riding that particular bus or van. Have one adult who is in charge of checking the roll as each person boards.
2. Have small groups of five, with a youth in charge of each small group. Call the list of "in charge" youth, who are responsible to know if everyone in their small group is present (also have an adult "in charge" of the adults).

CELL PHONES

Compile a list of the cell phone numbers of the youth on the trip. Give each adult a copy of this list. It might be helpful sometime during the week.

Give each youth a list of the cell phone numbers of the adults on the trip. They should have this list at all times but particularly during times that the group is separated. Have additional copies of the list to distribute to any who misplace their list.

T-SHIRTS

Consider having a special T-shirt designed for each tour. Select high quality, energetic, and colorful shirts that youth are proud to wear. These T-shirts serve not only as tour remembrances, but also as advertisements all year when young people wear these shirts to school. Involve choir officers in the shirt design process.

ROOMING AND HOUSING

Consider having the choir change roommates during the tour. Changing roommates helps youth get to know persons in addition to their best friends, and it helps to lessen the effect of cliques that might exist in groups.

STAYING IN HOST HOMES

If members of the choir are staying overnight in homes of members of a church, be sure that each youth has a card with the phone number of at least two adult leaders of the group to be contacted if there are any problems or questions. Group leaders should also have a list of where each youth is being housed, with addresses and phone numbers. Youth should also be given a "thank-you card" with instructions to write their hosts a thank-you note before leaving the home the next morning.

YOUTH MINISTRY RULES

In the same way that both parents need to have the same rules, so too does the youth department and the music department—especially on retreats and tours. Rules regarding appropriate dress, swimwear, and kinds of movies viewed should be the same for all youth trips, regardless of the staff person in charge. Ideally, these rules are discussed and adapted by a youth council so that they are rules that the youth themselves have decided are appropriate.

RETURNING TO THE REAL WORLD

A short talk the last day of tour on "returning to the real world" is helpful to students and adults. Include suggestions such as:

Resolve to treat your family with love as you return. Those on tour often return home tired, and we easily snap at our family. Resolve to show love.

When friends ask you "How was tour," use this as an opportunity to share something good and significant. Our tendency is often to say "Good" or to share some bit of gossip. Resolve to share something positive, meaningful, and spiritual.

FUND-RAISING

More and more, it seems that churches are discouraging fund-raising by groups within the church. However, some situations do require that massive amounts of money be raised to help pay the costs of a tour. The list of fund-raisers is limitless, of course. Wrapping-paper sales, fruit sales, bake sales, spaghetti dinners, garage sales, and singing telegrams all are good possibilities.

At Brentwood, the one fund-raiser for youth choir trips is the Share the Spirit auction. It has become an all-church event and involves persons of all ages, not just parents of youth. The auction is the only youth choir fund-raiser, and it raises enough money in one night to take care of the costs for summer tours.

Having a chairperson and a steering committee of highly motivated and committed parents is crucial to the success of the auction. The co-chair of the event is the chair for the following year, and every committee is set up in the same manner.

The auction includes items donated by local businesses, large dinners hosted by Sunday school classes and other persons, weekend and week-long use of lake cottages and condos, golf outings, art work, and many other items. Neither used items nor consignments are accepted.

There is a silent auction prior to the dinner and a live auction with a professional auctioneer following the dinner. At the beginning of the dinner, the youth choir sings several pieces, and through their music, the Spirit of God becomes a part of this special night. There is very little talk at the auction about the trip itself but rather about the opportunities for ministry that will be a part of the trip.

SHARE THE SPIRIT AUCTION ORGANIZATION
- Chairperson
- Co-chairperson
- Treasurer and Co-treasurer
- Committees (each with a Chairperson, a Co-chairperson, and members):
  - ❏ Acquisitions
  - ❏ Silent auction
  - ❏ Set-up and take-down
  - ❏ Dinner
  - ❏ Youth involvement
  - ❏ Publicity
  - ❏ Decorations
  - ❏ Table reservations
  - ❏ Ticket sales
  - ❏ Programs
  - ❏ Thank-you notes
  - ❏ Props
  - ❏ Live auction

Covenants

A covenant is a promise that holds spiritual implications. Covenants are promises that a person makes with God, with the adult leaders, with the other youth who are a part of the group, and with himself or herself. A covenant is much stronger than a contract, for it is a promise that we have made not only on an intellectual basis, but also, most important, with our heart and soul.

Directors and youth leaders must be willing to enforce the covenant. Although it can break the heart of a loving youth leader, we best serve the offending youth, and the group as a whole, if we enforce the rules and consequences in the way that we have said that we would.

The remaining pages of this chapter are examples of covenants. They can be adapted to fit specific groups or events. The most effective covenants are written by the entire group, or by the leadership team or officers.

It is good to have one covenant that the youth sign as a part of the registration form for a retreat or for a tour, and another covenant to sign on the day that they leave on the trip. Signing the covenant on the day they leave, and allowing each youth to place his or her covenant on the altar of the church, helps reinforce the young person's understanding of the importance of this promise.

Another kind of covenant is the covenant young people make in joining the choir. Consider using the Service of Commitment, illustrated at the conclusion of this chapter, at the beginning of a new choir year. The service can be enhanced by having the senior pastor speak, by having choir members share with each other how being a part of the choir has brought them closer to God, and by offering time at the altar for choir members to pray their own personal prayer of dedication.

COVENANT

I will allow God to use me on this tour.
You can count on me to give my best to God, to the other members of the choir, and to those for whom we sing.

I understand that I will get only as much out of tour as I put into it.
Choir members who contribute the most will get the most out of the tour experience.

I understand that being prepared for tour is my responsibility.
Being faithful and on time for rehearsals, "performances," and other events
Giving my best effort and best attitude to every rehearsal, "performance," and other events
Committing myself to helping the choir achieve the highest possible level of choral excellence

I also promise that I will not do things that will pull me or our group down.
I will not sneak out after curfew at night. (Those who do so will stay with counselors.)
I will not bring, buy, or drink alcohol, publicly or privately. (You will be sent home.)
I will not smoke, publicly or privately. (You will be sent home.)
I will not be a complainer.
I will not participate in any sexual activity. (You will be sent home.)
I will not gamble.

I understand that although the Rooming Coordinators have done their best to place me with my choices of roommates, this is not possible every night, and being with different people is a way to reach out to others.
I will make the best of every situation and will keep a positive attitude.
I will be kind and considerate of my fellow choir members and counselors throughout the trip.

A Covenant for Behavior on Tour

"The body is a unit, though it is made up of many parts, and though all its parts are many, they form one body. . . . Now you are the body of Christ, and each one of you is a part of it!" (1 Cor. 12:12, 27 NIV)

1. When listening to CD players, you must use earphones.
2. Safety is a major issue. You must always be in groups of two or more; do not go anywhere at any time by yourself.
3. Being on time is CRUCIAL. You must be on the bus on time, with your luggage loaded, because we have a schedule that is very tight.
4. Please carry with you at all times emergency phone numbers where your parents can be reached (home and/or work), and the cellular phone numbers for the adult sponsors.
5. The Covenant you signed is a promise to God and to other members of the choir. You will be sent home for violation of the rules.
6. While on the bus, please put trash in the garbage bag, not on the floor.
7. Do not bring any food or drinks into a church sanctuary.
8. Please commit to being in bed by midnight every night. God made us to need sleep to function at our best.
9. Every day, the first thirty minutes of the bus ride will be Quiet Time. Each of you will be given an awesome devotion to read and to think about. Also during this time, announcements will be made.
10. Although there are a lot of fun events during choir tour, our reason for going is to share the love of Christ through awesome singing, and to help each other to grow strong in our walk with Christ. Each one must work to help create a holy atmosphere on tour—loving, self-sacrificing, giving, and striving to be Christlike.

A SERVICE OF COMMITMENT

LITANY OF THANKS

Leader: God, thank you.

Choir: I thank you for the community who has gathered together, with many faces and many examples of your presence.

Leader: I thank you for the many people in this choir who give of their talents to serve your people.

Choir: I thank you for the hymns and songs so wonderfully prayed and sung for your glory.

Leader: I thank you for the gift of your saving Word, for planting your seed of love within us.

Choir: And I thank you for the mission that you have called all of us to accept— to be ministers through music, to sing with spirit and voice, and to usher persons into your presence through the power of music. For this I give thanks. Amen.

PSALM 100

Men: Sing with joy to the Lord! Worship the Lord with gladness. Come before him, singing with your whole being.

Women: Acknowledge that the Lord is God! He made us, and we are his. We are his people, the sheep of his pasture.

Men: Enter his gates with thanksgiving; Go into his courts with praise. Give thanks to him and bless his name.

Women: For the Lord is good. His unfailing love continues forever, And his faithfulness continues to each generation.

A PRAYER OF COMMITMENT

God,
I thank you with all my heart,
that you have blessed me with the gift of music.
Help me to always remember
that this ministry is important and special.
I pray that the notes and words on the page
will be the song within my heart.
Help me and my fellow music ministers
remember that we are not only performing music,
but we are also worshiping you.
Being a part of our choir is both a wonderful opportunity and challenge.
Help me to be committed to our ministry together. Bless each person here, and bless our witness together. Amen.

CLOSING PRAYER

Sample Tour Registration Form

CHOIR TOUR REGISTRATION FORM

NAME _____ PHONE _____

ADDRESS _____

CITY/ZIP_____

E-MAIL ADDRESS _____

CELL PHONE _____

MOTHER'S CELL PHONE _____

FATHER'S CELL PHONE _____

SCHOOL _____ GRADE IN SCHOOL _____

BIRTHDATE _____

CHOIR PART: Soprano   Alto   Tenor   Baritone   Bass

Will you need to join tour late or leave tour early? _____

If yes, be specific._____

Will you sing Home Concert? _____

Will you miss any of rehearsal week? _____

HEALTH INFORMATION

Is it imperative that you be in a home with no dogs or cats? (Which) _____

Are you allergic to any drugs or foods? (Please list)

_____

Will you be taking any medication during the trip? (Please list)

_____

Please list any health or emotional problems that the adult leaders need to be aware of:

_____

ROOMMATES

If there are people that you would like to room with during choir tour, please list them:

1. _____   2. _____

3. _____   4. _____

You will be put with at least one of these persons during tour; however, one of our goals is to help you get to know persons you do not already know.

EMERGENCY CARE MEDICAL FORM

Singer's Name _____

Address _____

City _____ State _____ Zip _____

Home phone _____

Singer's cell phone _____

Father's name _____

Father's work number _____

Father's cell number _____

Mother's name _____

Mother's work number _____

Mother's cell number _____

Singer's birthdate _____

Singer's Social Security No. _____

Parent/guardian Social Security No. _____

Family doctor _____

Address _____

City _____ State _____ Zip _____

Family doctor's phone no._____

Hospitalization insurance: Name of Company _____

Group No. _____ Contract No. _____

Policyholder's place of employment _____

List any allergies: _____

List any medications you are presently taking:

_____

Have you had any serious illness in the past year? _____

List any physical or emotional conditions the adult leaders or a
physician treating you should know: _____

CHAPTER TEN

WORSHIP

Now the LORD *came and stood there, calling as before, . . .*
And Samuel said, "Speak, for your servant is listening."
—(1 Samuel 3:10 NRSV)

"Choir has been one of the most important and influential
things in my life. Not only have I become a better
singer, but I have become a Christian."
—Letter from a member of the choir

Praying with the Youth Minister

Praying with the youth minister is not, obviously, a worship experience for the group; it is, however, a great way to worship with the youth minister, to deepen the bonds between these two ministries, and to set an example for the youth who are in the choir and youth group. Consider sending the following letter to several youth each week, and then setting a time each week to pray with the youth minister.

Dear Kara,
  You are being prayed for this coming week!
  This year we are beginning at the top of our list of youth and praying for two persons from each grade each week. You are one of the twelve who is being prayed for this coming week.
  We are doing this because we care about you and because we

believe that there is real power in praying for others. Our prayer is that you will feel the presence of God in your life, and that you will ask God to be with you in all that you face.

If there are specific concerns or problems that you would like us to pray about, please give either of us a call. We are here for you and want to help you in any way that we can. Feel free to come by any time!

We hope that you have a great week! See you on Sunday!

Your Friends,

Contemplative Spirituality

Contemplative spirituality is worship that is characterized by an atmosphere of quiet beauty with candles and crosses, prayer, scripture, gentle guidance in listening for the Spirit, and individual options for connecting with God. Young people, I believe, are hungry for quiet, beauty, and time to connect with God. Contemplative worship is never manipulative, and the emotions it draws from young people are real, not hype. Almost all of the worship services suggested in this chapter are contemplative in nature. Some general options for worship times include:

1. Quiet Time. Give time, particularly at the beginning of the day, to go outside. Furnish a sheet of paper with directed meditation or directed prayers, or provide space for them to write their own prayer, and so forth.

2. Prayer Room. At retreats, set up a small room with atmosphere, paper and pencils, a cross, and chairs for prayers at any time.

3. Prayer Partners (for retreats and tours). Adults and college students sign up to be prayer partner for a specific youth who will be on the retreat or tour. These persons write a letter to the youth, sharing their faith journey and their favorite Scripture. These letters are given to each youth during a worship time on the tour. Later in the week, each youth writes to the prayer partner, sharing about the tour and their experiences during the week. It's a great way of connecting adults and youth, and involving adults in praying for youth.

Worship Services Based on Prayer

THE CHAIR

Set up a large, dimly lit room with candles, quiet music, and one to three chairs in the center of the room (lots of space between chairs). If you have a small group, one chair is best; a large group needs three. The group enters (can be singing "Sanctuary" or another quiet song), forms a big circle around the room, and are seated on the floor.

Begin by singing songs to set the mood for worship. The leader talks about the power of prayer, the power of being prayed for, and the power of praying for someone else, that we are a family, and we want to pray for each other, that every one of us has hurts and challenges in our lives. The leader then invites the youth to take a risk and allow persons to pray for *them*.

One youth volunteers to be seated in a chair and then *no more* than three persons are asked to come and place their hands on that youth and pray for him/her. The worship leader explains that we may or may not know the specifics of what is going on in each life, but we can still pray for the person. After a minute or two, one of those praying at the chair will need to say a brief prayer out loud (just loud enough for those around that chair to hear), and then all return to the circle. As each chair is vacated, someone new comes. During this time, everyone in the circle can be praying silently for the persons in the chairs.

Consider asking two or three people to be "starters"—the first ones to the chairs. This service can be intimidating at first, so it is helpful to have youth ready to "model" being in the chair.

After the worship leader senses that everyone who wants to be in the chair has come, invite the group to share their experience either of being prayed for or of praying for someone else to do so. Again, have a couple persons pre-arranged to begin this time of sharing.

After a few minutes of sharing, invite everyone to stand and put their arms around the shoulders of the persons next to them in the circle, to look at the person on their left, and at the person on their right. Everyone in the circle then bows their head, and the leader says a pray, including these words: "God, hear us now as we pray for the person on our left (then silence); now hear us as we pray for the person on our right (silence)." Conclude this time with a brief prayer.

SABBATH STATIONS

Sabbath Stations is a powerful service of prayer. Give each youth a copy of the descriptions of each station, which serves as a road map for the service. Each station requires blank note cards, pencils, and baskets for receiving the cards. Some stations can be enhanced with a cross or candle, and some require additional materials.

After a time of explaining the service and a group prayer, instruct the youth to go to whichever stations they feel led, and to spend as much time as they want at the various stations. Allow about thirty minutes for this service. Play quiet music. Conclude with a time of sharing.

A few years ago, a young man in the choir shared these words: "For four years I have participated in the Sabbath Stations. Each year I have gone to the Word of God station, and each year I have drawn the word *trust*. I can't help but believe that God is speaking to me, and tonight, I want to trust God." Contemplative worship opens the path for youth and the Spirit of God to communicate.

The Sabbath Stations service rests in the power of each person taking time to talk with God and to listen to God. The following material can be copied for each person to use as their personal guide for this worship service.

The Sabbath Stations

SABBATH is a time to rest . . . to stop.
SABBATH is not simply a day off . . .
it is the presence of peace that happens when we
give
mindful
attention
to ourselves and to God.
Jesus said:
Make your home in me, and I will make mine in you.
Take all the time you need.
Go to the stations where you feel led.
TAKE YOUR TIME.
PRAY SLOWLY AT EACH STATION THAT YOU GO TO.
Sabbath is a time to stop . . . and to give mindful attention to
ourselves and to God.

EMPTYING MYSELF

Before we can really be open to the Spirit of God, we need to
empty ourselves of "possessions" and things that are holding us
back from being open to God and to others.

*Write your name on the bag provided. On the back of the bag, write
any worries and concerns that you need to leave behind for a few minutes so that you can be free to listen to God. Place in the bag everything
in your pockets, all your jewelry, and your watch. In this way, you
symbolically empty yourself so that you can listen to God. Place the
bags at the front of the room before you go to the other stations. After
you have spent time at all the stations, you may pick up your bags.*

1. THE WORD OF GOD

In taking time to meditate on a word or phrase from God's
word, we are often able to be open to hear God's message for us.

*Take a card from the basket. Say the word or phrase that's on the
card over and over. Then listen to what God might have to say to you.
Be quiet, and say the word or phrase again several times. Allow this
word from God's word to accompany you tonight.*

2. GRATEFULNESS

Our world encourages us to constantly think about what we do not have. The world tells us that we need always to buy something newer, or bigger, or better. But God encourages us to find peace through gratitude.

Take your time. Think about the blessings of your life—of persons who care about you, of persons through whom you've seen the Light of Christ, of the ways in which your needs and wants have been provided for.

Take a card and write on it the things that you want to thank God for. Place it in the basket and slowly say a prayer of thanks to God.

3. CONFESSION

So much of what keeps us from having peace in our lives is our sense of guilt. Sometimes simply taking time to say aloud those things for which we are sorry begins to cleanse us and opens us to the light of God.

Take a card and write on it honestly those things with which you are struggling and for which you need forgiveness.

Say a prayer asking God to forgive you and to help you to forgive yourself. Then take a candle and carefully burn JUST A PART OF THE CARD OVER THE BOWL, symbolically saying that you are allowing God to forgive you, asking God to help you to forgive yourself, and asking for God's help in resisting the temptations of the future.

4. COMMITMENT

"The ways of the Lord are perfect, reviving the soul," says the Bible. True SABBATH happens when we are in right relationship with God and with others. At this station, you are asked to commit your life to God. Ask God to live in your heart, to help you to be a follower of Christ, and to be a witness of God's love to others.

Walking with Christ is a journey. It's a decision that we make over and over during our lives. Perhaps you need to make a commitment for the first time, or perhaps you need to re-commit yourself to allow Christ to lead your life. Write your commitment to God on the card. Say a prayer asking God to be the Lord of your life.

5. SERVING OTHERS

God asks us to be his hands on Earth. He asks us to serve others. Who do you need to serve? Your parents, your family, your friends, people in this group, strangers?

Write on the card the names of persons that you need to serve. Say a prayer asking God to help you live a life serving others.

6. RECONCILIATION

Reconciliation is an old word that means "to get in right relationship." Grudges or petty arguments or misunderstandings block us from peace, or Sabbath.

You are invited to join with whomever you need to reconcile. Talk in the midst of the candle, which symbolizes the Light of Christ. Commit your relationship anew to being the Light of Christ in each other's lives.

EVERY PICTURE TELLS A STORY

"Every Picture Tells a Story," published by Youth Specialties, is a collection of compelling photographs.[1] Each youth chooses a photograph, spends some time in quiet reflection, and then shares why they chose that photograph, the story that they believe is contained in the photograph, and how they see the presence of God in the photograph and story.

PALANCA

Palanca can be an awesome experience, both for the doer and for the receiver. The energy of Palanca prayer can make a difference in what happens on a retreat or tour.

The Palanca forms and the names of all choir members who will be on a retreat or tour can be available at a table in the church for two or three weeks prior to the retreat or tour. At the beginning of the retreat or tour, tell the choir that every person is being prayed for by name by someone "back home," and that "palanca" is being done in the name of this prayer. At the end of the retreat or tour, distribute the forms letting each youth know the person and event behind the Palanca that was done in their name. The following is a sample form for Palanca:

PALANCA

Palanca is a Spanish word that means to apply a small effort to achieve a great lifting power. "Doing Palanca" is a special way of praying that is used to assist people in making a major spiritual effort; it is prayer with an action component. The first part of "doing Palanca" is to complete the enclosed form and place it in an envelope with the name of the person assigned to you on it, and put it in the Palanca box. These brief notes will be given to the youth during the retreat.

The second part of "doing Palanca" is to pray for the person assigned to you, and then to do *something* to back up your prayer. For instance, you may choose to fast by skipping a meal, or you may do a special act of kindness for someone, or you may make a financial gift to a cause, or you may go to the church for a specific time of prayer. There are many actions that could reinforce your prayer.

PALANCA
Prayer with Action
(To be turned in and then distributed to the person for whom you are praying at the end of the retreat)

Dear _____,

I am praying for you during this retreat weekend. My prayer is that you will feel God's presence in your life in a very special way, and that you will come away recommitted to be a person that God wants you to be.

The "Palanca" (action) behind my prayer is:

In God's Love,

_____

Additional Worship Events

MORNING WATCH

An example of a Morning Watch is given following this paragraph. The Morning Watch is a devotion that is duplicated for each youth to use at the beginning of the day. Allow a few minutes of "alone time" for each young person to read the devotion and to ponder the meaning for his/her life.

SAMPLE MORNING DEVOTION

Let us begin this day with singing. Whether we feel like it or not, let us make glad sounds and force ourselves to express to God words of thanksgiving and praise.

The facts are: God is with us; this world and we who live in it are his; he loves us. This makes us valid, worthwhile. We are truly significant in the eyes of our God, irrespective of our human feelings or the comments of our critics about us.

SAMPLE MEDITATION

In whatever we face, God loves us and is with us! There are no secrets from God, who knows us and still loves us! When we hurt, God hurts for us. He is our friend. Read and reflect on this contemporary paraphrase of Psalm 23:

GOD, my shepherd! I don't need a thing.

You have bedded me down in lush meadows,

you find me quiet pools to drink from. True to your word, you let me catch my breath and send me in the right direction.

Even when the way goes through Death Valley,

I'm not afraid when you walk at my side.

Your trusty shepherd's crook makes me feel secure.

You serve me a six-course dinner right in front of my enemies. You revive my drooping head; my cup brims with blessing.

Your beauty and love chase after me every day of my life.

I'm back home in the house of GOD for the rest of my life.

(Psalm 23, THE MESSAGE)

LOVE FEAST SERVICE

The Love Feast is a powerful worship and group-building event. The setting of the room is important. Provide dim lights, candles, and quiet music. In the center of the room, have one to three tables, depending on the size of your group, on the floor. On each table place a white tablecloth, a loaf of French bread, a chalice with grape juice, and votive candles. Youth enter quietly and sit in a large circle around the room. After a solo and Scripture reading, give the following instructions:

> The Love Feast is not the Lord's Supper or Communion. It is a celebration of the love we share for one another through God. We use the symbols of bread and grape juice to remind each other of Christ's love for us, and how that love makes the love we have for each other special.
>
> "During the Love Feast, you may take one person, or as many persons as you want, to one of the tables to share the bread and juice. You may go as many times as you want. You may want not only to take your friends to the table, but also to reach out to those with whom you need to reconcile, or a person who is lonely and to whom you want to extend your friendship.

Encourage the choir maintain a worshipful attitude and spirit during the Love Feast. Put a time limit on the Love Feast of fifteen to thirty minutes, depending on the size of the group. Be sure to have plenty of juice and French bread to replenish the tables.

Worship Order

(*Enter to music; sit in a circle.*)
Solo
Scriptures (*to be read by various persons*)
Instructions for Love Feast
The Love Feast (*with quiet music playing*)
Sharing Time: "How have you experienced the love of God through the choir or persons on this trip?" or "What are your struggles? Where do you need support in your life?"

Closing—Prayer and Song

Love Feast Scriptures

Each of these Scriptures is read by a different youth at the beginning of the service.

1. My command is this: Love each other as I have loved you. Greater love has no one than this, that he lay down his life for his friends.

2. I no longer call you servants, because a servant doesn't know his master's business. Instead I have called you friends, for everything that I learned from my Father I have made known to you.

3. You did not choose me, but I chose you and appointed you to go and bear fruit—fruit that will last. Then the Father will give you whatever you ask in my name.

4. This is my command: Love each other.

5. If I speak in the tongues of mortals and of angels, but do not have love, I am a noisy gong or a clanging cymbal.

6. Love is patient; love is kind; love is not envious or boastful or arrogant or rude.

7. Love does not insist on its own way; it is not irritable or resentful.

8. Love does not rejoice in wrongdoing, but rejoices in the truth.

9. And now faith, hope, and love abide, these three; and the greatest of these is love.

10. My command is this: Love each other as I have loved you. Greater love has no man than this, that he lay down his life for his friend.

THE WALL

Construct a large wall with butcher paper on which bricks have been drawn. The wall, when erected, will ideally be about ten feet high and more than twenty feet long. At the beginning of the service the wall is put up in front of the worship area. It totally blocks the view of the cross.

During the service, the young people are invited to take markers and write on the wall things that separate them from God, from their families, and from others. Later in the service, one person should read Ephesians 1:14, in which Paul speaks of Christ tearing down the wall that separates us from God.

The participants are then invited to go and take pieces of the wall, which represent barriers in their own lives, as a way of affirming God's power to overcome this obstacle. The image of the wall slowly crumbling and the cross emerging behind it is a powerful image. At the end, the wall is gone, the cross is visible, and each person has a piece of the wall to take home to remind them of this service.[2]

GROUP SHARING TIME

Gathering in a large circle and sharing with one another is a deep experience for young people. Here are some suggestions for sharing:

1. Tell about a physical scar; tell about an emotional scar.

2. Enlightenment Candle—Pass a large candle person to person; person holding the candle says, "I've been enlightened with the realization that . . ."

3. "What I'm taking away from this retreat is . . ."

4. "I've seen God at work in . . ."

LETTERS FROM PARENTS

This event is built around each youth receiving a letter from his/her parents. Consider beginning this time by talking about how a parent's love is like God's love, and God's love is like the best of a parent's love. Then play quiet music and have each youth go to the back of the room where the letters are on a table. Each youth then goes to different parts of the room to be alone with his/her letter(s).

Come back together and allow those who would like to share to do so. Talk about surprises in the letters, funny things in the letters, and how the letters made you feel. Then, give each youth paper, pencil, and an envelope, and ask them to write their parents a letter in response. These letters then are collected and mailed immediately so that the parents receive the letters while their youth is still away.

Occasionally, there is a child with a difficult family situation. For these youth, I write a letter and ask siblings or other significant adults to write them. I have also learned that often the most powerful and important letters are the one received by young men from their fathers. A sample letter to parents is printed on the next page.

The following letter is sent to parents of choir members.

Personal Letter to Parents

Dear Parents of Choir Members:

One of the important and meaningful traditions of choir tour is a worship time in which we give each member of the group a letter from his/her parents. We are again doing this service on tour and need your *immediate help* in making it a great experience for these youth.

We need you to write a very personal letter to your child. You may write one letter from both parents, or, ideally, each parent will write a letter. In this letter you might want to:

- Talk about your love for your child.
- Mention the positive qualities that you see in your child.
- Talk about the positive growth that you've seen this year.
- Share something of what God means to you in your life and your hope that they also will remember God's love for them.
- Affirm your youth's involvement in choir and church.
- Pledge your total support as they grow through their teenage years.

Year after year, these letters are the highlight of tour week. All the youth, those who are very close to their parents and those who are not close, find these letters to be a tremendous affirmation and opening to new communication.

These letters are to be a surprise. We need your letter(s) by (*date*). They may be placed in the box in the music office or mailed to the church. Each letter should be sealed with your youth's name on the outside.

I know that everyone is very busy, and that this is one more thing to do. However, I know that it will be time well spent by you, and that it will potentially be a very meaningful experience for your child. Please keep this project a secret, and please have your letters to us by (*date*).

If you have any questions or concerns, please give me a call.

SENIOR NIGHT

"Senior Night" is a worship service in which we thank God for the influence and leadership of our seniors. It is a time in which we affirm each senior, and in which we pray for God's blessing on their life.

About two months prior to tour, I ask parents of each senior to work with their child to complete the form that asks for the names of two adults and two peers who have been influential in their senior's life. I then write these persons, requesting a letter to be written to the senior who has given me their name; I also ask parents to write a letter to their senior. All of these letters are returned to me.

On Senior Night, each senior is presented a notebook that includes these letters. The book also has blank pages so that it can be passed around and other members of the group can write notes of affirmation and thanks.

As each person receives his/her book on Senior Night, the floor is opened to anyone in the group to express to that senior how they have been positively influenced by his/her life. Hearing youth tell other youth that their morals are admired, that they are loved, and that the Light of Christ has shown brightly in their life is powerful stuff. The group is cautioned that this is a time for brief, *positive* sharing—no problems in a relationship are to be worked out in front of the entire group. Following the time of sharing for each senior, a member of the choir places his or her hand on the senior, and says a prayer of blessing.

Senior Night can take a lot of time, depending, of course, on the size of the group. It is, however, a meaningful time for each senior, and it is a time of powerful modeling for the younger members of the choir. I believe that Senior Night is one of the reasons that seniors stay involved in choir.

Another option, rather than opening the floor to all who would like to speak, is to ask each senior to name one or two persons prior to the trip whom they would like to speak on behalf of the entire group on Senior Night. Sample letters and forms for Senior Night are reprinted on the following pages.

Request for Senior Book Letters

Dear _____,

_____ has submitted your name as a person who has had a major impact on his/her life.

On our upcoming choir tour we will be presenting each of our seniors a book of letters. We want to include a letter from you as a person who is loved and respected by _____.

The letter might:

- Affirm your love/care.
- Affirm the positive traits that you see.
- List your hopes for the future as he/she finishes high school and begins college.
- Talk about how your relationship with this friend has deeply influenced your life.

If you feel comfortable sharing your faith and how it has been a positive part of your life, please include that as well.

WE MUST HAVE THIS LETTER NO LATER THAN (*DATE*)

Please mail your letter to me at (*address*).

If you have any questions, please call me (*give church and home phone numbers*).

Thank you for taking the time to write this letter. I know that it will have a positive influence on the life of your friend.

Sincerely,

Youth Choir Director

Example of Letter to Parents of Seniors

Dear Parents of Seniors:

As you know, we will be presenting each senior on choir tour a book that includes letters from adults and peers who have been influential in his/her life. An important part of this book is a letter from you to your child. You may write one letter from both parents or a separate letter from each parent.

The letter might:

- Affirm your love and care.
- Affirm the positive traits that you see and the growth that you've seen in his/her life.
- List your hopes for the future as he/she begins college.
- Talk about how your relationship with your child has influenced your life.

If you feel comfortable sharing your faith and how it has been a positive part of your life, please include that as well.

WE MUST HAVE THIS LETTER NO LATER THAN (*date*).

Please mail your letter to me at (*address*).

If you have any questions, please call me (*give church and home phone numbers*).

Thank you for taking the time to write this letter. I know that it will have a positive influence on the life of your child.

Sincerely,

_____

INFORMATION FORM FOR SPECIAL
SENIOR PRESENTATIONS

Senior's Name _____

Two Adults who have been influential in your senior's life who would be willing to write a special letter for this book. (We will contact them.)

1. Name _____
   Address _____
   City _____ Zip_____
   Phone _____
2. Name _____
   Address _____
   City _____ Zip_____
   Phone _____

Two Youth (peers) who have been influential in your senior's life who would be willing to write a special letter for this book. (We will contact them.)

1. Name _____
   Address _____
   City _____ Zip_____
   Phone _____
2. Name _____
   Address _____
   City _____ Zip_____
   Phone _____

If there are other adults or youth who have been influential, and you would like letters from them included in the book, please list their names, addresses, and phones on the back of this sheet.

RETURN TO: (_____ *name & address* _____)

BY: (_____ *date* _____)

121

LETTER FROM GOD

A copy of the following "letter from God" may be given to each youth. Time should be given for youth to go to a place (even in the same room) where they can read this letter. Provide paper and pens for each person to write a letter back to God. The youth can then place his/her letter to God on an altar or worship center. Mellow lighting and quiet music will enhance the spiritual mood in the room.

A Letter from God

I love you. I know everything about you, and I love you totally and completely.

There is no one at church, at your school, or anywhere in the world whom I love any more than I love you.

Even if you had been the only person on Earth, I still would have sent Jesus to be an example for you of how to love others more than yourself.

More than anything, I want to be close to you. I want to help you to make good decisions, to treat others the way you want to be treated, and simply to walk with you and to support you throughout your life.

Sometimes, because you are human, our relationship is not very strong. And because you're human, there are things you've done that have pulled us apart. I want you to know that there's nothing that you've said, thought, or done, for which I will not forgive you; all you have to do is to be sorry for what you've done and ask me to forgive you. And then you have to trust that I've totally forgiven you, and you must forgive yourself.

To keep our relationship strong, you must be committed to me (just as I am committed to you), and you must make me your number-one priority in life. Every day you must make a new commitment to our relationship and to doing your best to live your life as an example to others.

I would like to hear from you. Please write me a letter and let me know how you're feeling, how I can help and support you, and what you need to be forgiven of. I hope that you will also commit yourself to loving me every day.

I look forward to hearing from you. Remember . . . I love you more than you can ever imagine.

Love,
GOD

THE BRIDGE
"The Bridge" grew out of a similar idea used at Willow Creek Community Church.

For our "Bridge" service, the concept was that we must take a step toward God—we must walk across the bridge. There is something very powerful about actually walking across a bridge that makes "The Bridge" the effective service that it is.

The bridge used can be either one that is present at the place of the service or one that can be built and transported to the place of the worship service.

Communion

Services of the Eucharist can be a powerful part of retreats and tours. Consider a communion service before leaving, or as one of the worship experiences offered during the retreat or tour. Holding the service outside where youth are reminded of God's greatness through nature, or shared in small groups, or offered in the beauty of a great sanctuary, are ways of helping this service to be one of the most meaningful of the trip.

Worship Before Leaving on Tour

Load the bus, and then "begin" the tour with worship. I suggest that worship be held in the sanctuary, for this is our holy place. Consider inviting parents of tour participants to be a part of this service. Invite the senior pastor to lead this worship time. In his or her remarks, the pastor can both affirm and challenge the youth who are a part of this trip. We always allow time for the youth and parents present to pray at the altar, and we conclude this time by joining hands in a circle and having one of the youth pray. Other options for this "sending forth" worship include serving communion, signing covenants for behavior and placing them on the altar, and having each youth write three goals for the week and placing them on the altar.

Worship Leadership

Worship and group times on retreats and tours can be led by the choir director, youth minister, youth, or adult sponsors. Sharing the leadership of worship and group building times is, in most situations, the best plan. I believe that it is important for youth to experience the choir director as a person who cares about the role God has in their lives. It is also important, however, that they experience the youth minister, other youth, and adult sponsors as persons who care about the spiritual needs of the group. Leading worship is a gift—some are better at it than others; develop this gift in others and call upon them to share this gift with the choir. Consider forming a youth worship team who help plan and facilitate worship on retreats and tours.

Additional Resources

Ideas for additional worship experiences that connect with youth can be obtained from books and articles related to the "emerging" worship movement.

Notes

1. *Every Picture Tells a Story* (Grand Rapids: Zondervan, 2002).
2. The concept for the wall is found in *Deepening Youth Spirituality* by Walt Marcum (Nashville: Abingdon Press, 2001). This book is an amazing resource for youth worship.

PEOPLE

CHAPTER ELEVEN

GUIDING

But the greatest of these is love.
—1 Corinthians 13:13*b* NIV

The universal language is pain, not love.
—Anonymous

Like each of us, every youth in our choir room is dealing with a mixture of joys and struggles. Alcohol, drugs, depression, spiritual confusion, self-esteem issues, sexual issues, family issues, pressure to be great students and championship athletes, lack of sleep, pressure to live up to the expectations of well-meaning parents, teachers and church leaders, issues with absent parents, divorce, blended families, and peer pressure are all alive in the youth of our choirs. Sometimes the ones in the most pain are the ones we least suspect: class presidents, star athletes, and leaders in our choirs and youth groups; these youth sometimes feel great pressure to achieve and sometimes give themselves fewer "breaks" to not be great at everything.

Youth choir directors are always in the caring business. From time to time, young people may look to us for "spiritual listening." Here are a few suggestions for this important part of our ministry:

1. Be a good *listener*. Ask leading statements such as "Tell me more about that."
2. Be very selective in offering solutions. Leading statements such as "What options do you see?" or "What do you think you need to do?" are often the most helpful responses.
3. Remind them of God's love and care.
4. Be honest, but be careful about offering judgmental comments.
5. Hold confidences. Only share the information if there are life-threatening activities being experienced or if suicide is being threatened.
6. When talking with a person, keep the door slightly open. If something feels "not right" or inappropriate, end the session.
7. Do not try to be a counselor. Refer persons with deep problems to a professional counselor.
8. At important life moments, such as the death of a loved one, accidents, hospitalizations, or other difficult situations, go to the person in need. Your presence at the funeral home or hospital will be appreciated and will always be remembered. Presence is always more important than what one says.
9. I have found that students who graduate out of our youth choirs often look to us for advice during their college years; some of the most important conversations I've ever had have been with college students who were once a part of the youth choir. Consider writing a letter to each student at the beginning of their first semester at college, letting them know that you are eager to stay in contact with them, and that you are available to them if they need to talk.
10. Ultimately, I think that most persons simply need to be heard, to know that there are options, to know that they are not alone, and to be reminded that they are loved by God as they are.

CHAPTER TWELVE

MAINTAINING PASSION

*It takes courage to grow up and
turn out to be who you really are.*

—e. e. cummings

Although burnout is a huge problem for many persons who work in the church, I have found that an even greater problem is "brown-out"—that is, persons who still function and do the job, but for whom there is very little joy and passion for their work. Much of our struggle with brown-out occurs due to several factors: (1) issues resulting from our childhood and life experience; (2) the unique issues in ministry in the institution of the church; and (3) the challenges associated with the changing society in which the church exists.

I have found that those of us who are musicians and ministers are often dealing with seven common challenges: avoidance of conflict, fear of failure, chronic disappointment, low-level "simmering" anger, exhaustion, loneliness, and inflated ego. Dealing with these issues, which are all a part of burnout or chronic brown-out, requires personal insight and usually a wise friend or professional counselor to help sort out the personal, professional, and spiritual issues of our lives.

Even as we give ourselves in ministry to others, our life—both the good and the bad—is still happening. If we are going to effectively care for others, and if we are to truly thrive, we must also take care of ourselves. There are some things we can do to help us avoid "brown-outs" and to help us thrive in our ministry:

1. Set goals that are challenging but realistic.

2. Keep the vision of ministry clear. Our call to ministry is *not* to have the largest youth choir in town or to have every youth love us, or any other *unhealthy expectations we may place upon ourselves*.

3. Get to know the youth in your choirs. Knowing the joys and pains of individuals in your choir will help you to enjoy the choir at a deeper level.

4. Keep a "blue file." My friend Chip Colee shared this idea with me years ago. He suggested that we put every positive note that we receive into a folder marked "blue file." When I'm having a rough week, I go to my blue file and read some of the notes I've received over the past year. My guess is that you will be surprised at how many affirmations you actually receive in a year or two. Having this file helps us remember that there have been many wonderful moments in the past, and more wonderful moments will happen in the future.

5. Read good books. The resources at the end of this book include suggestions of many amazing books. There are great ideas, inspiring concepts, and helpful information available to us through books.

6. Attend conferences that expose you to new ideas and new music. For youth choir directors, the Youth Cue Roundtable each year is an excellent place to network with other directors, to get new ideas, and to gain new perspective on this work. Youth Choirs, Inc., founded by Randy Edwards, is a great resource for directors of youth choirs.

7. Keep first things first—God, family, church. Many of us are guilty of often putting the church first and our families and our own spiritual, emotional, and physical health last.

8. Have a person, or persons, with whom you can be honest. Share your frustrations with a person who can listen and can help you regain a positive perspective.

9. Take breaks. It's important for each of us to have other interests in our lives besides the church. Take your day off and take your vacation days; being away, even for part of a day, helps us to be a better leader when we return.

10. Find ways to recharge yourself spiritually. Regular Bible study and dedicated prayer time, journaling, and other spiritual disciplines are *required* for those who are in ministry. Consider being a part of a weekly small group experience (maybe create a small group with other staff persons in your church or with staff persons from other local churches).

11. Exercise, even moderate, is a great stress reliever. Exercise helps us physically and emotionally.

12. Determine whether a problem is an *event* or a *pattern*. For example, poor attendance at one or two rehearsals is an event; consistent poor attendance over a period of eight weeks is a pattern. Events and patterns deserve different reactions.

Passion

Passion is the enthusiasm in our heart and soul for something or someone. Passion connects us with our "calling" as human beings. Stephen Covey describes passion as "that with energizes your life and gives you your drive. It is the fuel at the heart of vision and discipline. It keeps you at it when everything else may say quit."[1] Passion is the belief in our soul of the importance and goodness of something or someone—even when it doesn't necessarily all make sense. Sometimes a youth choir may seem to not be worth all the challenges and frustrations that it may present. Hold on, however, to the reality that God's presence, combined with the power of music, the church, friendship, and being a part of something bigger than ourselves is a holy thing.

Two Young Men

Abe Graham was an eleventh grader who joined the choir at the invitation of a friend. Six months later, Abe was diagnosed with cancer; eight months after that, Abe died. During that time, Abe remained faithful to the choir. We were his church family. The anthem "Lord, Make Me an Instrument of Thy Peace" by Jody Lindh (Choristers Guild) was composed in memory of Abe.

Curt Williams was an amazing tennis player and a great guy. For whatever reason, Curt refused to join the choir until the beginning of his senior year in high school. But once he joined, Curt gave himself 100 percent to the work of the choir. Choir tour at the end of that year was a fantastic experience for Curt and his dad told me that Curt connected with God in a very important way on that tour. A year later, while a college student, Curt was killed by a drunk driver. The choir sang at Curt's funeral, and his dad spoke in the service of the importance of Curt's one year in the choir.

What is amazing about Abe and Curt is that in both cases, they were in the choir one year or less. Their time as a part of the choir affected each of them in profound ways. It is, in many ways, because of people like Abe and Curt that I remain passionate about the importance and power of youth choirs to transform young people.

Arkansas basketball player Patrick Beverly, in his team biography, said: "My passion for the game is one of my biggest assets."[2] What is true for basketball players is also true for youth choir leaders—our passion for the "game" is our biggest asset. Ultimately, it's all about passion, for passion leads us to keep going, to give our best, and to trust that God is at work.

Notes

1. Stephen Covey, *The 8th Habit* (New York: Free Press, 2004), p. 76.

2. ARSonline.com.

ACKNOWLEDGMENTS

It is with gratitude that I say thank you, and dedicate this book to: the hundreds of Brentwood United Methodist Church teenagers who participated in our youth choirs over the years; Karen McCarty and Patsy Wade, amazing accompanists who are also awesome people; the parents of youth who raised the money and served as sponsors on retreats and tours; the best senior ministers any church musician could ever hope to work with: Bishop Robert Spain, Bishop Joe Pennel, Dr. Ben Alford, Bishop James King, and Dr. Howard Olds; the outstanding youth ministers who have served Brentwood Church; members of the music staff who also worked with the youth choir ministry, particularly Betty Bright and Beth Teegarden; and to James Wells, who now leads this ministry.

In addition, I want to thank students in my classes at Belmont University who gave input on much of the original material and to directors of youth choirs around the country who have encouraged me, taught me, and whose choirs inspired me. Thanks also to Ty Webb, Mark Hagewood, and Jean Merritt, each of whom typed and corrected various forms of this manuscript over the years, and to Debi Tyree and Julianne Eriksen, whose editing and patience vastly improved this book.

Resources

Choral Conducting

Jordan, James. *The Musician's Soul: A Journey Examining Spirituality for Performers, Teachers, Composers, Conductors, and Music Educators.* Chigago: GIA Publications, 1999.

——. *The Musician's Spirit: Connecting to Others Through Story.* Chicago: GIA Publications, 2002.

——. *Evoking Sound: Fundamentals of Choral Conducting and Rehearsing.* Chicago: GIA Publications, 1996.

Neuen, Donald. *Choral Concepts: A Text for Conductors.* Wadsworth, 2002.

——. *Empower the Choir!* Choral Excellence, 2003.

——. *Choral Techniques and Methods* (a series of seven DVDs). Choral Excellence, 2002.

Sharp, Timothy W. *Precision Conducting: The Seven Disciplines of the Masterful Conductor.* Leawood, 1996.

Willetts, Sandra. *Beyond the Downbeat: Choral Rehearsal Skills and Techniques.* Nashville: Abingdon Press, 2000.

Warm-Ups

Jennings, Kenneth. *Sing Legato: A Collection of Original Studies in Vocal Production and Musicianship.* Kjos, 1989.

Seelig, Timothy. *The Perfect Blend: Over 100 Seriously Fun Vocal Warm-ups.* Nashville: Shawnee Press, 2004.

Tefler, Nancy. *Successful Warm-Ups.* Kjos, 1995.

Leadership and the Church

Covey, Stephen. *The 8th Habit: From Effectiveness to Greatness.* New York: Free Press, 2004.

Hybels, Bill. *Courageous Leadership.* Grand Rapids: Zondervan, 2002.

Lencioni, Patrick M. *The Five Dysfunctions of a Team: A Leadership Fable.* San Francisco: Jossey-Bass, 2002.

Lundin, Stephen C., Harry Paul, and John Christensen. *Fish! A Remarkable Way to Boost Morale and Improve Results.* New York: Hyperion, 2000.

Maxwell, John. *The 17 Indisputable Laws of Teamwork: Embrace Them and Empower Your Team.* Nashville: Thomas Nelson, 2001.

McLaren, Brian. *The Church on the Other Side: Exploring the Radical Future of the Local Congregation.* Grand Rapids: Zondervan, 2000.

McManus, Erwin Raphael. *An Unstoppable Force: Daring to Become the Church God Had in Mind.* Loveland, CO: Group Publishing, 2001.

McNeal, Reggie. *Practicing Greatness: 7 Disciplines of Extraordinary Spiritual Leaders.* San Francisco: Jossey-Bass, 2006.

————. *The Present Future: Six Tough Questions for the Church.* San Francisco: Jossey-Bass, 2006.

Stanley, Andy. *The Next Generation Leader: 5 Essentials for Those Who Will Shape the Future.* Sisters, OR: Multnomah, 2003.

Youth and Youth Choirs

Dean, Kendra Creasy. *Practicing Passion: Youth and the Quest for a Passionate Church.* Eerdmans, 2004.

Edwards, Randy. *Revealing Riches and Building Lives: Youth Choir Ministry in the New Millennium.* MorningStar, 2000.

Mueller, Walt. *Engaging the Soul of Youth Culture: Bridging Teen Worldviews and Christian Truth.* Downers Grove, IL: InterVarsity Press, 2006.

————. *Understanding Today's Youth Culture.* Tyndale, 1999.

Spiritual Reading

Bell, Rob. *Velvet Jesus: Repainting the Christian Faith.* Grand Rapids: Zondervan, 2005.

Job, Rueben P. and Norman Shawchuck. *A Guide to Prayer for Ministers and Other Servants*. Nashville: Upper Room Books, 1983.

McManus, Erwin Raphael. *Seizing Your Divine Moments*. Nashville: Thomas Nelson, 2002.

Miller, Donald. *Blue Like Jazz: Nonreligious Thoughts on Christian Spirituality*. Nashville: Thomas Nelson, 2003.

Nouwen, Henri J. M. *Can You Drink the Cup?* Notre Dame, IN: Ave Maria Press, 1996.

———. *In the Name of Jesus: Reflections on Christian Leadership*. Crossroad, 1989.

———. *Life of the Beloved: Spiritual Living in a Secular World*. Crossroad, 1996.

———. *The Way of the Heart: Desert Spirituality and Contemporary Ministry*. New York: HarperCollins Publishers, 1981.

Peterson, Eugene H. *A Long Obedience in the Same Direction: Discipleship in an Instant Society*. Downers Grove, IL: InterVarsity, 2000.

Books by Coaches—Leadership and Motivation

Holtz, Lou. *Winning Every Day: The Game Plan for Success*. New York: Harper, 1998.

Jackson, Phil. *Sacred Hoops: Spiritual Lessons of a Hardwood Warrior*. Hyperion, 1995.

Krakauer, Jon, *Into Thin Air: A Personal Account of the Mt. Everest Disaster*. New York: Anchor, 1997.

Krzyzewski, Mike, *Leading with the Heart: Coach K's Successful Strategies for Basketball, Business, and Life*. New York: Warner, 2000.

Pitino, Rick, *Success Is a Choice: Ten Steps to Overachieving in Business and Life*. New York: Broadway, 1997.

Riley, Pat, *The Winner Within: A Live Plan for Team Players*. New York: Putnam, 1993.

Summit, Pat. *Reach for the Summit: The Definite Dozen System for Succeeding in Whatever You Do*. New York: Broadway, 1998.

Youth Worship

Norman, Jonathon, Gavin Richardson, and Brandon Brooks. *Worship Feast: Creating Unforgettable Experiences* (CD-ROM). Nashville: Abingdon Press, 2006.

Marcum, Walt. *Deepening Youth Spirituality: The Youth Worker's Guide*. Nashville: Abingdon Press, 2001.

Middendorf, Jon. *Worship-Centered Youth Ministry: A Compass for Guiding Youth into God's Story*. Beacon Hill Press, 2000.

White, Daniel S., Jonathon Norman, and Beth Miller. *Worship Feast: 50 Complete Multi-Sensory Services for Youth*. Nashville: Abingdon Press, 2003.

White, Daniel S., Jonathon Norman, and Jenny Piper. *Worship Feast: 100 Awesome Ideas for Postmodern Youth*. Nashville: Abingdon Press, 2003.

Worship Feast Prayer Stations: Creating Unforgettable Experiences (CD-ROM). Nashville, Abingdon Press, 2006.

Important Web Sites

Center for Parent/Youth Understanding: www.cpyu.org (one-stop information on youth culture).

Youth Choirs, Inc.: www.youthcue.org (interdenominational resource for youth choir directors).